FLIPPING HOUSES

The Best Real Estate Investing To Buying, Rehabbing And Selling Properties For Profit Even With No Money

Table Of Contents

Disclaimer

The material contained in this book is provided for educational and informational purposes only. No responsibility can be taken for any outcomes resulting from the use of this material. While every attempt has been made to provide information that is both accurate and effective, the author does not assume any responsibility for the accuracy or use/misuse of this information. Some names have been changed and/or omitted in order to protect the privacy of certain characters in this book.

INTRODUCTION

Many years ago, the word "flipping" wasn't a household term, only a few people related the word to properties and profit-making. People never wanted to sell their properties, even in the worst circumstances and they only sold if it was their last resort, until the economic recession in the United States made a lot sell their homes to survive. Recently, not only house builders, contractors, electricians, and carpenters make money from houses, but some young entrepreneurs also make money from real estate even without having any knowledge of the profession. These people are called house flippers. Flipping is a lucrative business with a mouthwatering salary; however, it is also risky and can be stressful if things didn't go as planned.

There is a cordial relationship between flipping and real estate, but flipping is used to describe short term real estate transaction. The term flipping is a process that deals with the purchase of an asset and selling it out. In flipping, the investors acquire assets, add improvement of some kind, control them and sell within a short period for profit. Flipping applies to stocks, shares, and real estate. In other cases, it can also be used for cars, sports tickets and concert tickets. The primary aim of any form of flipping is to make a profit. Flipping can be done in politics, IPOs, technical trading, professional fund, management, car, and real estate. IPOs mean Initial Public Offering. IPO happens when the shares of a company are made accessible for the public to own/purchase. Most companies sell their property cheaply during this period and this is to ensure that the property is quickly purchased. The people that buy IPO shares and sell them out to make a profit are referred to as IPO flippers. For real estate, flipping has an offensive meaning as it is believed that it is used to describe an investor that buys a house at miserable amounts or lowest possible price with the intention renovate to boost its value. That is, it is related to manipulation in the market which may be associated with socially destructive and unethical activities, fraud and dulling people of their properties to make huge profits. Flipping is also applicable in macro funds that require the use of broad market trends. The managers of macro funds may decide on flipping sectors where they sense potential losses and divert the gains to profitable sectors.

However, in recent times, most people have viewed real estate flipping as a respectable and regular business. Car flipping has also made ground and it refers to the purchase of a car at a cheaper price and selling it at a higher price. The people who are involved in this act are referred to as car flippers and they are trained at bargaining prices for flipping both buying and selling of the properties. However, this book is limited to the house flipping.

CHAPTER ONE

HISTORICAL PERSPECTIVE

1.0 The History of Real Estate

When, where and how did the real estate start?

Real estate history differs from country to country, men and women rate of selling houses depend on the country they transact business. Who could ever think that people have been investing in real estate before the revolutionary war, is it true? The first real estate which was recorded was found in the cave drawings. The caves weren't rented out to tribal Homo Erectus as the incorrect history of landlords stated out. Rather, it was verified that there was a currency exchange among ancient people to obtain shelter. When property right was developed, real estate took another phase as it created the first "defensible property". Real estate marketing became very popular in the middle age and many people depended on it as a source of income for their livelihood. In those days, even up till date, the owning of a property is seen as a symbol of wealth and it has been viewed as a way to acquire wealth. Ever since the middle age, the real estate business has flourished. Real estate business is economy sensitive and should be treated as one.

People in the United States weren't left out in the real estate investing, started presenting houses for sale around 1900 and it is still up till date. The improvement in the economy during the 1920s brought about a rush in the real estate business, especially for houses. However, there was a declination in the economy in the mid-1930s which made about 16 million people unemployed and real estate demand was greatly affected. The first real estate transaction in the United State started in 1890 but the association which was attempted to be formed failed. Another attempt was made to raise an association of real estate in 1908 and then the National Association of Real Estate Exchanges was founded which connected the real estate agents to know the principles required in real estate business. Even with the presence of an association, anyone could refer to themselves as a real estate broker until 1919 until it became an offense to refer to yourself as a real estate broker without a professional certificate to show for it. The reason for this was due to the dubious act that was inculcated into the real estate business by the amateur. Investing in real estate became popular in recent years which have been traced to occur due to the rise in the value of properties and decreased interest rate. The real estate industry might have been developed by our ancestors; the zeal for selling of property for financial gain was pushed by the driving force related to this evolution. During the 1980s, "The Old House" a television program which originated home programs on the television gave rise to other programs by other TV stations and this has improved the knowledge of real estate by the populace. The TV shows have mainly featured programs such as home repair, DIY projects, how to flip houses and factors to look out for when purchasing a house. The effect of economic recession on real estate cannot be overemphasized as houses are always under foreclosure and stocks are always held down. With the growing process real estate had to go through, it had resulted in financial freedom and paved the way for profitable property investment which has been enjoyed by some Americans.

The Inhabitants of Australia have long been involved in the sales houses but recently, real estate brokers have been able to have formed an association with respect to home sales real estate agents began as individual entities without a body but in 1981, a group was created where the real estate agents in Victoria converged to discuss investing in real estate. The association led to the creation of the "First National Group of Independent Real Estate Agent Limited" was created. Within 30 years, these groups had become the best real estate group in Australia. The United Kingdom has the largest or second-largest real estate in Europe after Germany. The Chinese developed an interest in real estate investment after seeing the United Kingdom prospering in the act and were encouraged by the support the United Kingdom government gave the real estate investors in its country.

1.1 History of House Flipping

Having known that house flipping is a branch of flipping which constitutes the major part of flipping, I think we must know how it began and what prompted people to think they can buy a property (house), rehab it if necessary and resell it to make a profit. Also, how did it come into the limelight? About 30 years ago, people were only exposed to buying and reselling of house, only a few people understand the term "house flipping" unlike today where the word house flipping means something no matter how little to someone. All of these occurred due to the publicity created by various TV shows and at present, the term is known.

Historically, house flipping has been occurring since Colonial times and even before America became settled. Owning a property is ranked among the highest symbol of wealth in the pre-colonial England and one of the main ways to establish property taxes was to know the amount of wealth a person is worth House flipping was done by a selected people who were rich and had the resources coupled with the knowledge to carry out the exercise. The main move that established house flipping was the recession that occurred in 1980 which held down the stock market earnings and increased the number of foreclosures of some homes. Another precursor of house flipping was the establishment of Federal Real Estate Investment Trust (REIT) legislation in 1960. Although the legislation had been adjusted over the years, it paved way for a larger real estate industry as the expansion of any industry enables the search for a larger market. Therefore, today, there is enough space for house flippers to spread their wings and explore. However, in recent times, house flipping is now open to lots of people and quite a reasonable knowledge about it has been passed on through social media and all other communication networks.

In the 1980s, there was an economic recession which affected a major population of the United States. House foreclosure became very high and people who could buy foreclosed homes at low prices and fixed them up with their own money and watched as the market improved where they resold it for a reasonable profit which was the main history of house flipping in America. People began venturing into the business in 1990 and renovating ancient homes became popular. Various shows such as "This Old House" and Bob Vila the media celebrity educated people on the reasons they should take up the renovation or flip rather than demolishing a house they own. Would you rather renovate or demolish a house you own and continue living in it or rather flip it to get your dreamed one?

Most people will go for the former as it's a house they have once owned and would prefer to keep it to themselves, but a young entrepreneur will always settle for the latter. However, house flipping isn't only about getting a house, renovating it and reselling it. It is way far above that and to be a successful house flipper; the first thing in history is to know how to purchase a house at a very affordable price that would be profitable.

One of the factors responsible for the popularity of house flipping is the knowledge and popularity of the renovation of old houses. Since the time people have been exposed to the renovation of houses, house flipping has been on the high side. Television programs such as "This Old House" of about 1980 has given rise to more similar programs which have made a lot of people experts in house flipping.

CHAPTER TWO

WHO SHOULD READ THIS BOOK?

Have you ever imagined buying a property and then selling it to make money or have you always been interested in real estate management? Then you didn't stumble on the wrong book.

Now the big question: *who should read this book?* While writing this book, so many factors and people into consideration. We all know that flipping business is a risky one and when taking risks, we need a percentage of reassurance that it will all work out. This book has been designed in such a way that many of our questions and doubts are sorted out in it.

The first set of people who must lay their hands on this book are those who are considering a career in flipping properties. If you find yourself always wanting to watch the home renovation programs without being bored, then you might be a house flipper. There is a huge guarantee that you would earn a great deal which comes in relatively fast and easy if you do all that is required of you.

If you don't know the exact things to expect in flipping, then this book should/must be a part of your library and reading it must be on your to-do list. Not everyone is a real estate expert and in house flipping; we need to attain a good level of professionalism. The cost of buying, renovating, level of profit and for selling is the major factors of house flipping.

Entrepreneurs who want to try out flipping and require their knowledge. I can reassure you that confining yourself to TV programs might not give you the required knowledge of flipping. But before you face the reality of it, this book will not only focus on the profits and benefits you derive from flipping rather there is also information on the risk and disadvantages of flipping.

However, flipping is a great business to venture into and when done appropriately, you will never regret trying it out.

CHAPTER THREE

WHAT TOOLS DO I NEED?

Like every other profession, house flipping also requires tools to maintain its management. There are must-have tools every house flipper must have whether they are just taking up the entrepreneur skills of being a house flipper or they are already a seasoned house flipper. To be highly successful in this field, you should always keep yourself on the availability of new tools, improved ways of doing things and the best ways to get things to do things that can make your house flipping unique and profitable. There are both online tools and physical tools. The following are important software tools that every house flippers or real estate investors must practice.

3.1   House canary

This is a tool that aids investors to understand the true value of the property. It is an online data and analytics platforms created as an app majorly for this purpose. This platform database contains immediate or present housing information which helps you predict the returns on an investment in a home using the predictive analytics engine. It helps to determine whether it is safer to buy a house for rent or flip it. The app was created with reverence to two people. The first is for a person who is new in the investment business and doesn't know how to manually estimate the likely profit from to be obtained from a particular property. The old investors aren't also left out as the app help them give a more professional sight on how to present their case to a potential lender rather than relying only on their method of analyzing profits via spreadsheet. Every real estate investor needs to explore houseCanary and testify to its effect.

3.2 Dealmachine

When there are too many investors on a particular property, the price tends to be on the high side. Dealmachine has come to rescue you by helping you but properties no one else knows it is for sale. This is also an online app that gives information and enhances you buying off-market properties that are equally a good deal. For instance, assuming you saw a desolate property and you feel the house will make a good property for flipping. Capture the house with your phone camera using your dealmachine app, the app will instantly pop up the information about the owner of the property. I think things have been made easier from there but the function of dealmachine doesn't end there. You can continue by sending a postcard to the owner by letting them know your interest in buying the house. Dealmachine is a far easier way to get transactions done and helps you to get properties to purchase and flip easily.

3.3 Call Porter

Missing phone calls as an investor is like losing a customer, therefore, answering phone calls is as important as owning a phone. But it quite impossible not to miss some calls and that is why call porter app was developed. It helps to answer your calls. It is an app that has been specially designed and trained to fix appointments and help you serve your investors right. It is programmed in such a way that the software recognizes the caller and the lead had a personalized experience with the person. You can always listen to every call made when you are available.

3.4 Magicplan

The magicplan is designed to help you dig in a little deeper on the profit or approximated time for rehab on the property you are interested in flipping. The magicplan has great influence such as:

First, it makes use of the picture of the property you took to generate an Augmented Reality floor plan. It goes as far as providing the measurement of the every, the level of flooring required, the painting that is needed and all you will need if you want to renovate the house. You don't have to bother yourself on the cost of materials too as magicplan will also take it up from there. When you have magicplan, you can always take a picture of the house you want to flip and within seconds you know all that is required to the place.

3.5 Property Fixer

Property fixer has made itself known as "the ultimate tool used for real estate investors who are flipping properties". Whenever you are scouting for houses to flip, this app could be a useful one to always go with. The property fixer is a good flip analyst. When you spot a property that looks great for flipping, property fixer works when you input the basic information about the property into the app. The app comes up with a flip analysis that shows the estimate on profit and gives back potential on the investment.

3.6 Realeflow

This a business management design specially created for real estate investors. This app is used to trace deals, manage contracts and use emails to get information on current market strategies.

3.7 Repair Estimator Plus

To avoid a total waste of time which can due to lack of enough resources or not meeting up to expectation, you need a tool that can help to determine if a property is worth your time and available resources, this tool helps you to estimate the cost for a particular deal and helps to create a document that is presentable to potential lenders.

3.8 Matterport 3D

You must fill this app all by yourself. When you have a house you want to sell, all you need to do is make a video tour of the final product while you focus more on the improved and captivating part of it. You are assured that calls won't stop coming in and buyers won't seize knowing on your door.

3.9 Houzz

This helps locate local professionals that are referred by trusted clients. With this, you can learn from them and have more experience, this app can also aid in discovering beautiful design ideas and give tutorials on some DIY exercises and direct you to where you can shop for good and reliable home materials.

3.10 Redfin

Redfin is a very good tool for comparing comps in an area. It is specialized in comparing the local competition in an area and help you to look for the best market strategy that can be useful for you. If you have made up your mind to hire the service of an agent for the sale of your house, then the redfin is prepared to stand by you and make the search easier.

3.11 SPYFU

In any field you find yourself, you must make yourself known as the best especially in the entrepreneur game. That is, you must market yourself and make people know what makes you different from the rest and the reason they should do business with you. This is one of the secrets of success in entrepreneurship. Spyfu elevates your site by aiding in the tracking of keywords, stalking your competitors and analyzing the exact ground you are on.

3.12 Carrot

Real estate business has always been regarded as a business between people, but recently, working on making your investment known is equally as important as your need to try to connect personally. Carrot is used to provide reliable and fast-growing websites for real estate investors and agents. Real estate investors can make use of their websites in various ways. You can decide to set up a website where the right types of seller and buyers are collected at an affordable fee.

3.13 Dealcheck

Most investors want to be certain of the deal they are getting into before putting up their butt into it. The best deals for estate investors are when they buy the property at a cheap price, spend less on renovation and sell at a high price. However, sometimes when you feel you have hit the deal on the head by getting the property at a good price, but you lose money on renovation will cut down your wings. Therefore, it is more important for you to work well with your contractors and estimate the repair cost. If your cost of constructing goes a lot above your budget, your profit is at stake. So dealcheck helps you to make estimate the cost of repair and forecast the profit you should expect on a deal made.

3.14 REIPro

In all entrepreneurship activities, there is a lot that has to do with customer service and customer relationship management is of utmost importance. Most times in real estate business, you deal with customers directly and the relationship you maintain with them goes a long way even up to referral point. Investors are the major builder and agents of maintaining the relationship with people even after you deal with them is closed. Sometimes from the investor's end, there is always a loss to follow up with their clients which is majorly the investor's fault as clients tend to forget they were even transacting business with them because they have failed to keep in touch. When you are on the top list of people, they decide to come to you quickly when they require your service. Al you need is a relationship and trust. Majority use CRM systems that allow you to set reminders and save automatic outreach while REIpro does all of this and keeps the interest of the investor in mind.

3.15 Patch of Land

Having an app to learn and improve about investment is very important but having funds to secure and buy it is equally important. Most banks and mortgage lenders do not often want to lend real estate investors loans and those who want to give out give cumbersome application process that takes a long time than most investors could wait for. In this case, an online platform such as Patch of Land can be helpful. A Patch of Land is a nationwide money lender to majorly house flippers. The online platform lets you submit your investment loan in within minutes and you get your loan within days.

There are times you need to do some things all by yourself. If this is to happen, then you have to consider some must-have tools such as: hammer, magnet, wire stripper, large level and small level, power tools, screwdrivers, measuring tapes, stud locator, chalk string, gloves, putty knife, paper towel, shop towels, garbage bags, magic eraser, tapes, paint brushes, rollers, pans, vices and pry bar.

CHAPTER FOUR

FUNDS IN FLIPPING

There is a popular saying among investors that "*it takes money to make money*". Even before you make the decision of venturing into flipping, you should know the basics that every house flipping business commences with the lookout for a property to flip, once you have gotten that, you need money to buy the property which is just the beginning, there are holding cost of the home (which include insurance fees, HOA, and other home-owning costs) in cases where a rehab is necessary, materials would be purchased for renovation, to close it up, there is realtor cost, agent cost, and closing cost which also requires additional money. Therefore, flipping is all about money, money, and money. The more you can invest, the more you expect back in return. Fortunately, you have an option because there are multiple ways you can source for fund for your fix and flip business which allows you to purchase your property and do the necessary things that are required and then you sell out, get your profit and pay back your quota. Unfortunately, it isn't as easy as it sounds.

There are various ways flippers can get fund to work with but since the downturn that occurred in 2008/2009, the process for funding has been way rigorous and more cumbersome and you need to demonstrate a high creativity skill to get what you want.

You need to be enlightened and know the funding patterns that work for you before going ahead to apply for a loan. When you have a piece of good knowledge on these things, it will speed up your borrowing process:

4.1 Make a Business Plan for Every Flip

In flipping, you need to fix houses that are not in good condition. In the case of lending money, you must estimate the amount of money that would be required to finish up your project. This business plan would be given to the lender on the loan you are applying for. Your business plan booklet doesn't need to be voluminous; it only needs to be comprehensive and neatly detailed.

Your write up should consist of the following:

1. Address of the property
2. The cost of homes in the environment
3. Timeline, budget plan and financial cost of the renovation
4. Business partner and their background information
5. Plan B in case the renovation doesn't work as planned.

4.2 The Cost of Renovation

To avoid borrowing less money than required which can greatly affect your project, you need to create a well detailed and comprehensive range of work before concluding on the amount you are sourcing for. Let there be an outline of all the repairs that would be carried out on the property you want to flip. Your scope of work is very necessary for this step. You can't just sit back and make your scope of work; you need the service of professionals such as contractors and experienced appraiser. These parties will inspect the site and estimate cost of materials that would be required to put the property in good shape including the cost of labor. The scope of work must also consist of loan-to-value (LTV) and after-repair value (ARV). The LTV includes comparing the size of the loan to the value of the property. The greatest LTV value is around 90%. ARV is the estimate of the value of the property after renovations are made.

4.3 Spread Your Tentacles

Your connection in real estate determines how far you go. A financial connection is very important to get funds. Inexperienced investors can find it hard to get people to trust them with their funds, therefore, to make things easier, join your Local Real Estate Investors Associations (REIA) to interact with other investors and get connected. Most experienced and wealthy real estate investors do both, they apply for loans for their investment and give out loan for people's project. So you cannot underestimate your local investors.

The following are places you can source for funds for your flipping business.

4.4 Loan from Family and Friends

We have emphasized on how important connection is in real estate investment. When you have a one-on-one connection with people, great things are about to happen in your flipping business. Your relatives or friends could eventually be your flip lender because you have a good and trustworthy relationship with them or sometimes, they can refer you to people who can invest in your project. Some people are interested in real estate but do not have the time or knowledge to lead the crew, therefore, they would gladly invest in your project. Since you have a direct connection with your lender, therefore there is a sure deal that your interest rate will be minimal and affordable.

There are some things to consider and put into practice when getting loans from family and friends. First, remember to put the terms and condition regarding any loan in writing to avoid future argument and to maintain the cordial relationship among everyone. In the agreement book, the interest rate and payback period should be recorded and adhered to strictly. Secondly, all IRS and security laws should be applied to the family and friend loan. Third, let the lender know how real investment funding works and that he should expect his money until the house is sold.

4.5 Private Investors/ Hard Money

Hard money!!! Sounds scary. Well, you should also look at the part where it is written as private investors. Hard money is the money gotten from private investors. They are loans that are not obtained from banks rather they are gotten from private investors. Some rich individuals might want to own a share in real estate projects but aren't ready to stand alone or do the engagement required in real estate themselves, therefore, they take up the option of lending out money to those that are interested. It has lower requirement before it can be obtained unlike the bank loan and it can be received within the space of two weeks. Hard money can also be derived from friends and family who are interested in real estate projects but lack the patience and expertise required in the business. Getting fund through hard money is quite a scarce and an expensive option, you can only be lucky if you have wealthy friends or family who are also willing to invest checked and reviewed by a real estate attorney who understands every terms and condition and explains them to you as well as the consequences if you are unable to complete the project at the appointed time. Be sure of the interest rates, the manner of payment and the consequences that await if the project fails before venturing into hard money lending.

4.6 Get a Financing Partner

This means of funding is best for people who are experienced in house flipping and have deep knowledge of how to get a perfect finance partner. A partner in the flipping business does not only contribute his quota of the money but also helps in making the project a success. A finance partner can engage in the search of a property to flip, the planning and management of the property for renovation and the major thing (finance). In most cases, the profit is based on each partner's contribution towards the project or they can come to a compromise on how the profit would be shared. Sometimes in partnering, a partner takes charge of the fund while another searches for flipping opportunities. Your decision to stick to just one person as your partner or change partners for each project is personal. Just as you would do family and friends, every agreement and terms should be documented appropriately.

4.7 Personal Loan

Although, getting personal loans can have a deteriorating effect on your credit card, nevertheless, it gives you a payment schedule that is predictable and particularly to loans have a fixed interest rate. A personal loan is very suitable for people who have good credit and only need a small amount of money. In most cases, if you think your credit card and personal income are on the high side, you can always apply for a personal loan that can use in your flipping projects. Most lenders require your credit card having about 620 and above to ensure you can pay back the loan. A personal loan is a very flexible means of financing.

4.8 Credit Cards

Credit cards are a very good bet when we are sourcing for funds. It has unique characteristics of being fast, reliable and flexible. It is cost-effective when for short term loan but can have an interest rate of 12 to 21% or higher in the long run. The option of using a credit card for real estate funding requires creativity and a bit of science. It works well and is less stressful when you have good credit and a sufficient income to back it up. There are various ways credit cards operate and they are listed below

- Cash advance: some credit cards are designed to allow you access an advance form of cash which entails a higher interest rate when compared with purchase. You can also be eligible for a cash advance fee of 2% too.
- Balance transfer: some many agree on low rate balance transfer. Where you can use one to pay the balances you have incurred.
- Supplies: some credit cards are used to buy the materials needed for the job. If you are opportune to purchase the close of your credit card, you can increase your cash flow by

getting interest-free use of the card for almost two to three months.

4.9 Mortgage Financing

it might be difficult to get a traditional mortgage to use in purchasing a property, all the same, you don't have to mislead lenders on your intentions towards the property you want to purchase. There are times you buy properties and decide to stay in it for a while before you resell, let every intention you have towards any property you want to purchase be made known to the lenders to avoid questions. There are two types of mortgage funding investors use successfully. They include:

- **Cash-out refinances:** With a cash-out refinance, you will be able to use more than the current balance on the mortgage to refinance a property. There is always an extra fund that is, fund after loan costs which you can decide to spend as you choose.

- **Home Equity Loan:** Also referred to as the second mortgage is a type of debt that allows you to spend your cash on whatever you choose to you only pay interest on the cash you made use of. It is referred to as a fund gotten by tapping into the equity in your personal property. The amount of the loan is based on a comparison of the existing market value and the investor's mortgage balance. The in-home equity loan, your own equity share in the home will represent your collateral for the lender. The amount an investor s allowed access to be determined based on a combined loan-to-value ratio (CLTV) of about 80% to 90% of the value of the property. Traditional home equity loans have terms for repayment which will include the fixed payment including interest. To be fully qualified for a home equity loan, you should have reasonable credit and adequate monthly income which can pay off your mortgage and the home equity loan.

4.10 Financing

This is suitable for flippers who have enough wealth to kick-off or have enough retirement savings. However, it is very unsuitable for people who are approaching or close to retirement. You can decide to take a loan or withdraw from your 401(k) account. Younger people who have started saving can decide to use this method if the assurance of benefits outweighs the risk. In this method, you are almost taking a loan from yourself and then you also pay interest alongside the money, the interesting thing is that both the loan and the interest are paid back into your account, therefore, you they are all yours.

4.11 Fund from seller

This is also referred to as owner financing. Here, the seller of the property also stands as the lender. This is usually difficult as most homeowners wanted the money immediately and some also sold it for the money, they would derive from it. If the seller is interested in financing it, then it is a good move. Seller lending is very advantageous to both the seller and the buyer. The seller fixes a date (balloon date) in which the buyer must pay back the loan. The investors might have not been through with the project; therefore he must pay back personally or do through bagging other loans. As with every loan, all your deals should be in writing. It is also advisable that a lawyer is involved to draft and keep the loan papers.

4.12 Business Line of Credit

When you have been in the flipping business for long and you have a reasonable success history, then you can be exposed to bank financing. A business line of credit is a preferable option than a traditional bank loan for real estate investors for flipping. This source of funding exposes you to a specific amount of money, but you only pay for the amount you used.

This advantage makes the business line of credit the best option for you when you are not sure of the amount you would spend on renovation property and also, the interest rate is relatively low but you can only qualify to have it by having good credit. A business line of credit is like the home of equity in action, but the noticeable difference is the money you are exposed to. You can either apply for a commercial line of credit at your local bank or small business line of credit at Bank of America, Chase, Fargo, and Wells.

Buying a House with Your Own Money or Taking a Loan

As there are people who can afford to use their money to buy a house to flip so also there are people who only depend on loans to get their projects done. Asides the opportunity of having your own money, some people have their own money and still wouldn't invest into their house flipping business, rather they prefer to borrow and then lend out their money to other investors in the same business. Doesn't this sound weird, you could have just dug deep into your money for your use instead of having to go through the loan stress. Nevertheless, there should be a reason most experienced entrepreneurs do not use their own money for their house flipping. We can always try to analyze that

House flipping is a profit-making business and that doesn't require as much time as other high-profit businesses before you can get a reasonable profit. Most experienced investors have tried working trying both options of buying with their money or venturing into loans and they had seen a clear difference which is quite different from the reality we expected.

Experts have explained that flipping homes using your money is less profitable compared to when you get loans. Yes, it's not what we expected even after the interest and the attorney fees, signing for a loan is still as twice as profitable. Let's check out this analysis.

First, you purchased a house with your own money for $300,000 cash, the house was fixed for $50,000, then the renovated house was sold for $400,000. Real estate commissions and legal fees cost $25,000. The profit made on the deal was $25,000. The total amount you input into the project was $350,000. Therefore, the percentage of your profit is

The overall profit was above 7%.

Second, you obtained a short-term loan of $300,000 with a down payment of $60,000 you have a balance of $240,000. $50,000 was spent on renovation but $40,000 of that was borrowed. The renovated house was sold for $400,000 and real estate commissions and legal fees also cost $25,000. You decided to pay the bank 1% of the loan per month as interest and the deal lasted for 5 months making $14,000. So your financing cost was $14,000. Although the $25,000 you would have realized without financing became $11000.

This is over twice the margin. You don't have to go broke and spend all your life savings on house flipping when you other options that can work twice better.

For safety, it is safer to use you all your own money if you have it, but it is more profitable to get loans.

CHAPTER FIVE

UNCERTAINTIES AND RISKS INVOLVED IN HOUSE FLIPPING

Market economies have unlimited uncertainties. Unlike some other businesses such as house building, house flippers are also usually unaware of the problems awaiting them behind the walls or in the inner part of ancient houses. Experience of these expose flippers to the problems that may lie ahead, and those things can be put into consideration. Most house flippers face risks ranging from interest rate risk especially those on loans to the real estate market risk.

Uncertainties have a great power to change economic decisions and increase the uncertainty of expected incomes. Uncertainties increase when there is a financial crisis or after the end of a financial crisis in a country. House flippers try their best to get make sure the house can be flipped and at a reasonable price. Amidst all, there are various uncertainties that are the major factor which might occur just when you thought you are almost at the endpoint of the project.

These are the risk that you should always consider when you venture into house flipping.

Strategies to minimize risk and increase profitability

Market Development

Be sure of the happenings in the flipper's market, the development, and its movement. It's advisable you know if the market is favorable or set to boom flippers. Make inquiries from national sources or the local real estate agents monthly to avoid running at a loss after much work and consultations when just a phone call could have saved you from the mess.

Economy Shift

How is your economy? Is it stable or shifts with time? Is it declining or growing? You must lay your hands on all these pieces of information before you begin any deal. This will lead you on how to place your price either below or above. You have a lot of online sources where you can get these pieces of information; you are only a click away.

Rates of Interest

You need to keep monitoring interest rates. There are times when interest rates are expected to increase; therefore you must charge higher than normal to make a good profit.

Time

Although you can house flip at any time of the year, there are times you expect higher profit than other times. As an experienced house flipper, it is advisable you target those times of the year to maximize your profit. For instance, in late January, sales of homes are always low, and flippers have no choice than to sell it out at a low-profit rate to meet up loan payment. But during the middle of the year, sales rise to its peak. So, instead of flipping a house when sales are low, target and design your house flipping to meet up at the middle of the year.

Renovations Plan

Your renovation budget should outweigh the original price you are offered especially when you are on a loan. When you get this wrong, then your profit is gone, therefore, to avoid wasted effort, you must get this right and well. Make sure every renovation the house need is penned down and well inspected by professionals such as contractors and appraisers. You don't have to do irrelevant things such as the ideas of how you want your own home to be furnished. Instead, focus on the important things such as broken things and getting rid of outdated designs and updating the house to increase its price value.

Learn from Others

When you get to a crossroad and confusion sets in, don't waste time in calling the attention of your experienced friend in that field. There is a saying that "two heads are better than one" so they can always help you to get a solution to the problem instead of you trying to do more damage. This could occur in various aspects of house flipping, it could be while buying a property, rehabbing or trying to pay for commissions.

Know Your Ability

As a house flipper, know your skillset and the place where you are more comfortable to carry out your flipping business. Some house flippers are good with working with extremely old houses in a suburban setting while some can only work within not-so-old houses. Know your capability and do not exceed it to get the best result.

Contractors Problems

Even without house flipping, you can agree with me that getting a very good contractor that is also conscious of time can be quite challenging. However, to get the best out of a contractor, make sure your contract is worded consisting of the details of everything that is needed in completing the job. Do not let the contractor handle it alone, work also as a supervisor, input your own ideas too and try to correct errors immediately they are made to avoid expensive damage. When the contractor gets out of hand to refer to the written contract.

Potential to Lose a Reasonable Amount of Money

Every good thing has its own risk. Although the money you make in house flipping is mouthwatering and it comes quickly, so also can you lose a lot of money as fast as possible. These are various ways you can lose money:

- **Increase in tax**

There is a higher tendency that the city will increase a tax on a completed property. There might be a problem if you don't get a buyer early enough therefore, you must be responsible for the payment of the tax. It can also be a hindrance to the buyer's interest in purchasing the property due to the high tax bill. In some cases, you end up losing a good part of your profit to the payment of tax. Therefore, when you own a property you are supposed to flip for over a year, your capital gain rate will vary. However, there can be a chance for you to do a 1031-Exchange and delay the taxes to a particular time in the future.

- **Unknown or Hidden Pairs**

This shouldn't be strange to house flippers because almost all houses have this. There are times you try to remove previous doors, and, in the process, you find out the doorpost has more problem which is different from the damaged door. This is bound to happen in all homes and that leads to extra expenses especially when it was not expected. It could be a water problem on the roof or the bathroom. To avoid these problems on every repair, add a 1% contingency fee to every repair in your budget. If you do not use them, then your profit is higher but it's safer that way or in some cases, you end up spending all or some of it.

- **Holding Cost**

The more time you are holding onto the property; the more bills you must pay. Costs ranging from the mortgage (if you have a mortgage on the property), taxes, insurance, cleaning of the environment in some cases plowing of snow. These costs swallow up the budget and make you lose more money than expected. The best solution to this problem is to sell out the property early enough but no one wants to run at a loss.

- **Finding It Hard to Sell Out Properties**

After the buying and rehabbing of property, the most discouraging part of house flipping is not to get a buyer early enough. Every day from the day you completed the house and you couldn't get a buyer for it, you lose money. Your holding cost charges as long as the house is in your custody. When a house stays without being sold for a long period, you might eventually have to reduce its cost which will reduce your expected profit.

- **Stress**

It is an unarguable fact that house flipping is time-consuming and very stressful. Ever house flipper must have a plan B as things most times goes beyond the stipulated times and might not even come out as planned. There are times you do the wrong things; times contractors disappoint and lots more. When you keep having experience of these things, you eventually know how to handle them when they arise again, and you won't be put off balance.

CHAPTER SIX

HOW TO PLAN AND BE BETTER PREPARED

Your readiness to take up the challenge is what makes you outstanding in the field. You must be prepared for whatever lies ahead and be focused. A house flipping business plan would guide you and let you know the steps you need to take to make adequate profit. It is highly required regardless of the number of years you have been involved in the flipping business. There are tips you should always keep at the back of your mind and reflect on every time. They include:

- **Mission statement:** A mission statement defines your company's purpose. Your mission statement should be brief and self-explanatory consisting of the main activities you perform. In the case of house flipping, your mission statement should explain that you would fix up distressed properties and sell them which in the process employed is created and at the same time, neighborhoods are developed. Your mission statement should point out your houses of interest and the development you intend to make on them.

- **Summary of your goals:** A goal summary means summarizing both your long- and short-term goals and how you intend to achieve them. According to a rule of thumb that you should state your goals and explain the ways, you plan to achieve these goals and how you want to implement them and the time you think you can achieve them. Your goals can be categorized using time such as annual goals (these are long term goals and take a year), quarterly goals (these are short term goals that are joined together to make an annual goal and they are achieved four times a year) and monthly goals (these goals helps you achieve your quarterly goals and are done monthly).

- **Lead Generation:** After you have stated your goals, your next line action is how to achieve them. Lead generation can help, you will need to create a lead that would aid you to get properties that are for sale that you can flip. Leads can be generated via local real estate agents, creating bandit signs, online sites such as Zillow or foreclosure.com and going from door-to-door. You can also consult lead generation when you want to sell the fixed house. The more the number of people that know about your property, the easier it is for you to see it which is a good deal.

- **Comparative Market Analysis (CMA):** This is a tool can that give a person a price his property should be sold. It compares the number of homes sold in the environment and predicts a supposed suitable amount. The homes that are compared should have some similarities such as the same landmass, number of rooms, bathrooms and their important characteristics. The houses should also be close to one another. Most CMAs are usually carried out by real estate agent and they charge little or nothing if you have been working with them as a client. You can also decide to carry out the CMA yourself by going online to get records of previously sold homes and determine the sales price that is suitable for you. There are some things to look out for when performing a comparative market analysis and they include:

1. Make sure you compare only similar houses. Do not compare a 5-bedroom house with a garage to a 3-bedroom house without a garage.

2. Do not forget to take note of the environment. Never compare a property in an urban-urban area to a property in a rural-urban environment.

3. Do not overlook school district ratings. These are features can determine the price of property whether it must be increased or reduced.

4. Use sold prices instead of pending prices. The pending price has a greater chance of changing but the sold price is fixed.

Timeline

The timeline you have set is determined by how quickly you were able to get a property and how long you will take to renovate and the period it takes for you to sell it out. Your time frame has a direct impact on your budget and your market strategy and when you will move on to the next deal. If you are lucky enough, you can complete your flip within 2, 3 and 4 weeks, depending on the earlier stated factors. All you need to put at the back of your mind is that for every day the house stands as yours, you take responsibilities for the fees attached to it.

Budget

Your budget is a very crucial part of your business plan. It determines the amount you have assigned to each thing that needs to be done for your flipping to be successful. It includes the cost of getting a property, fixing it and selling it out. For easy access, I would highlight some important features that must be a part of your budget

1. Cost of getting a property
2. Closing cost
3. Estimated renovation cost
4. Marketing cost to aid the selling of the property
5. Staffing cost.
6. Carrying cost such as mortgage payment, property insurance, utility bills, and HOA fees if applicable.

Source of fund

Details on the source of the fund can be found in chapter two. You need to know where and how you will get the fund you will work with. Without money, business plans can't be executed. There are various sources of the fund if you don't have or do not want to use your money. You only must choose the best type of fund that works for you within the various means of sourcing for funds such as private loans, home of equity loans, family and friends or any other suitable funding avenue. Choose loans that won't take too long before they would be approved.

Exit strategy

This is how you intend to get your entire money after the whole fix and flip process. This is one of the parts that interest your lender most and it must be detailed. One of the best ways you can get your money back is to quickly flip the property and pay off the loan to move on to the next deal. Another exit strategy you can consider is a cash-out refinances. An idea where the flipper decides to refinance the property so that he can be entitled to equity out of the home. To achieve this, the investor pays the existing loan with the new loan and gets the difference in cash. Most flippers invest the new money into another property or use it to develop their old properties.

How to avoid risk

Avoid Homes with Impaired Mechanicals

When you are buying a property for fix and flip, it is advisable you buy properties that need only cosmetics improvements. Do not go as far as buying homes that need major repairs for electricity or a house whose entire roof must be replaced or in some cases, homes with foundation issues. Stay within your means, major repairs are costly, and they take too long to be completed.

Check the Property

Before you start bargaining on the price for a property, inspect the property. Buying properties not seen is a serious risk and in most cases, it doesn't end well. Therefore, before you decide to make a budget plan for a property, do adequate inspections to get an accurate budget.

Exit Strategy

Make sure you have other exit strategies aside from the fix and flip strategy. Every goal of a flipper is to sell the property quickly and move unto the next deal, however, there are some unforeseen circumstances that might make things out of control such as a shift in the economy, change in financing rules or difficulty in getting a buyer, then you have to look for other exit strategies before it becomes a burden to you or at the end of the whole deal, you can settle for cash-out refi or you own the house if it wouldn't have too much effect on you then you can sell it out when the market becomes more favorable.

Know Your Buyer

Another important aspect of house flipping is for you to know your buyer. Who is eligible to buy this property from you? This helps you to know the ideal price to tag the property and it gives you an idea of what to expect. It helps you to know the kind of renovation you should do, is the house designed for the wealthy or an average income earner or a low class. Spend your money wisely and create something you know would be sold in no time.

Have a Good Rehab Squad

Nothing works better for a first-time house flipper than a wonderful rehab team. The success of flipping lies in the combination of an honest contractor, trusted real estate agent and a mortgage lender. The collaboration of these sets of people gives an amazing output. An honest contractor will give the exact things needed for the rehab.

1. Choose the right market
2. When you choose the wrong market on your first deal, you will feel like you have done the whole thing wrong. When you know the market you are working towards, your renovation tends towards the market and the amount people will be ready to pay. Therefore, select a property that would be easy for you to sell.

CHAPTER SEVEN

HOW TO FIND A HOUSE TO FLIP

To be a successful flipper, you must find properties that are low enough to let you have a reasonable profit. There are various ways you can get a house to flip. If you want to get a house to flip, then you have two assignments to do. The first is choosing a market while the second is finding a property. Searching for houses to flip can be quite difficult but that doesn't mean you have to settle for anything that comes your way. The following are ways to get the property you have been looking for.

1. **Search the Multiple Listing Service (MLS):** the MLS is a database that was compiled by real estate agents consisting of all the properties that were put up for sale in a geographical area including their information and vital statistics. Access to the MLS is not free and it is only opened to realtors who have

registered to pay over $100 in a month. Those who are not realtor only gain access to this tool by aligning themselves with one or either as a member or partner or just for help. All you must be sure of is that the realtor you have chosen has access to MLS. In a recent market study, it was confirmed that more houses were sold on MLS than through owners directly meaning that the houses listed on MLS have a greater tendency of being sold faster than those not listed.

If a buyer isn't allowed to access MLS, there are other sites that also have information on homes available to be sold. The sites include Zillow.com, ziprealty.com and realtor.com. They are also well-known sites that have various house listing that is just as great, but they may not be as detailed as MLS. MLS is a very helpful tool that can be there for you during your search, however, it is still a tool and you can still use other means to secure a house to flip where you may even spend less. Now let's continue with the search.

2. **Link Up with A Real Estate Investment Group:** A few years ago, real estate investors groups have been quite popular, and it keeps making grounds in years. There is a higher probability that some of it will be in your local vicinity and you might not regret checking them out. They provide you with details and networking opportunities that might be of help in your search for a house. Also, houses that are available for flip are always enlisted in the monthly newsletter piled by these groups. Another means of connecting to real estate investors are getting familiar with many online platforms that can assist you in getting a property to purchase. Examples of such sites are biggerpockes.com gives detailed information on housing opportunities. There are also various sites on LinkedIn and Facebook that can be of help.

3. **Search for Auctions:** When estate and foreclosures auctions are on, they are opportunities you should grab for properties at a discounted price. Although you should be set for bidding wars though. If you do not depend on loans to get properties, then you are at an advantage of getting properties at sheriff's sale or the auction. Auctions are usually advertised weeks before, therefore, be on the lookout for. while reviewing the list, chose properties that fall within the auction period. Most auction properties cannot be well inspected as trespassers are prosecuted. The bidding wars too can be a disadvantage because people tend to buy it at a price that is above what they should have paid for because they were carried away with the bidding experience. So when you are bidding for a property, make sure you have a limit where you must not go beyond and stand by it.

4. **Classifieds:** Recently, people hardly advertise the homes they intend to sell on newspapers or put up for sale on their property. Although, some local newspapers still run adverts for property sales on paper or online. It is not usually seen as the best source for finding a property to flip. Going through the newspaper for adverts can be time-consuming because you must get as much newspaper as possible and it seems quite archaic in this digital world.

5. **Wholesalers:** Wholesalers are people who help house flippers get rehab properties. This is usually what they do as a contract, instead of you looking for properties to flip, they bring the properties that can be flipped to your doorstep. This makes property buying quite faster as the wholesaler acts as the middleman although the move is not cost-effective because you must pay the wholesaler for his service. There are a lot of

wholesalers who take this as a full-time job and are well connected to make your work faster. If you have chosen a wholesaler as your resort, you can get them from real estate groups or via the internet.

1. **Use an agent:** If it is your first time flipping or your first time in flipping in a new environment then an agent can be at your rescue to avoid frustration. An agent is an active way to make your search faster and appropriate. Agents know the right places to go at the right time which can make them give you various options instead of having to settle for what for you found due to lack of options. Agents who specialize only in real estates are your sure bets. They help you look for homes that are almost foreclosed or not well maintained by its previous occupants. These properties are usually cheaper due to the conditions they are making them suitable for a house flip. You can make your search online

by looking for REO real estate agents around a specific area.

2. **Location:** Location is a very important factor when you are trying to get a house to flip. One of the most determining factors that will add value to flipping your property is the place it is situated. It begins with the city, then the road, neighborhood, availability of schools and other social amenities. Also, other factors that should be considered when dealing with location is its proximity to places such as stores, public transportation among others. In some cases, figure out who the buyer of the property you are about to flip could be, which age group dominates the environment, if young couple dominates, then school becomes of great importance but if old people dominates then the school is less important. Is the environment rural or urban? If it is urban where almost all the inhabitants own a car, then proximity to public transport

is of less importance but where average income people are dominant closeness to public transport is very important. In case they all have cars, then the house you are buying to flip must have a driveway. You need to consider all these factors to aid your flipping process. Know who your potential customer can be, be familiar with them in your brain by the location and consider the same factor they will want to consider when they want to purchase the house.

3. **Condition of the property:** You will want your property to be able to market itself with its physical characteristics or be able to stand the local competition in the area. If you want to get off flipping a property quickly, then purchase a property that has similar characteristics with those in the neighborhood but along the process, don't do more than you can afford. When you make your property too exquisite compared to the ones you met in the

neighborhood, you might still have to sell it at the same price the small houses in the neighborhood are sold. Let your finishes and overall curb do the marketing. You can also make attractive engagements such as fencing or landscape, make the yard attractive. Dwell on what will make your property more attractive and what will make people want to get the house.

4. **Finance:** How far can your money go? When trying to find a house to flip, check your pocket and look at the numbers therein. As you know that you can never tell the exact amount you will spend on rehabbing a property, the only prices you can be sure of the amount you will get the property and the closing cost associated with the property. Every other thing will be a gamble. You can make a close estimation through professionals but be certain of unexpected expenses; it's the norms of rehabs. There are times the rehab

takes more time, the longer it stays, the more the cost. So you will agree with me that you must get a property within a closed budget. Houses within an environment sell within the same price range but do not overlook seasons. As earlier stated, that there are times of the year when house flipping sales are at their peak and there are periods when the market is hard, and prices are low. Have total control over your cost, do not do over your means, even if it's your money, endeavor not to go broke. Time management should be your watchword and you are on the path of having a great flipping.

5. **Adhere strictly To the Rules:** In obtaining loans lenders usually, put house flippers to the condition of lending between 65 and 70% of the after-repair value. The reason for this is that the house flipper's primary aim of doing the project is to make money, so when the cost of the property and the rehab costs above

65-70% of ARV, there is likely to be less or no equity for the investor to make money at the end of the project. However, there are still other costs that would eat into the equity, such as holding cost, insurance fees, taxes and so on. Follow the rules, lenders are only profited when they give out loans, so believe them when they say there is no adequate equity on a project.

CHAPTER EIGHT

FINDING A COMPETENT REAL ESTATE AGENT

Majority of homeowners make use of real estate agents when they want to sell or buy a house. Therefore, in a real estate transaction, choosing a good and competent real estate agent is very important. The best real estate you can always not regret working with are who are experienced and display some traits of professionalism by paying attention to your contribution and knows the market like the back of their palm. The agent doesn't have to work at the largest brokerage, done millions of transactions or be extremely rich. It is believed that only 20% of the real estate agents perform 80% of the business. Now, it is your duty to get search for the one out of the 20% to work for you.

Pay Attention to Neighborhood Signs

Track neighborhood for houses with for sale signs and put down the date it is being put up. Follow up until you stop seeing the signs or when the house was marked sold. Get information of the agent that sells listings fastest by following up with the number of listings put up in his name. You can get connected to such agent. Results speak louder.

Advertisements in Prints

You can try out your luck by checking newspapers or online searches for real estate agents. Agents advertise themselves for reasons. First, when they have an estate to sell, secondly, when they want to promote themselves. Go for agents who have properties to sell in your location of interest and contact them. They might be just the person you are on the look for.

Let's Ask Professionals for Recommendations

We all know that our first stop to consult for agents would be our family and friends but these people don't even know the exact features we are looking out for or how these things work so let's go more professional by asking experienced house flippers on the contact of good and reliable agents. They'd be glad to refer them to you.

There are questions you should as real estate agents before you hire them. These questions are important if you are really in search of competent agents. Even when the agents are referred to you, you shouldn't scrap the fact that you need to know their ability before you hire them or else you are on the verge of toying with a huge sum of money due to sentiment. Here are questions you can ask them:

Are You Experienced, If Yes What Experience Do You Have?

This question is designed to help you know how well they know the market and about the sale of properties. It is not necessarily connected to the number of years they have been an agent. Ask them the properties that have been sold in your area a few months ago. Request for the prices of properties that are similar to your area of interest. Ask them how they intend to discount you on the sale of a property. A good agent will not want to venture into the sale of an overpriced property. A good agent should also know at least something about everything in the real estate market. All you should focus on is how the agent can benefit you and not about the people he has worked with in the past.

How Do You Describe Your Marketing Plan?

In asking this question, the agent is expected to give you a comprehensive description of what he will do to make your property get off the market early. How creative is the agent, what will he do to make your property attractive and stand out among others? Let them show you how they have been able to sell properties in the past through their websites and the service of a professional photographer would be required, the one who can tell a story through a picture by capturing details and important aspect of the property. Unique features should be paid attention to.

Communication

Let the agent know your preferred mode of communication either via text, phone calls or emails. Agree on the time duration on sending reports on the progress of the sale of the property. Ensure the agent can be easily accessed in case of emergency or when you have a piece of information to pass across to them. Let them know how important it is for this property to be sold on time.

Agree on Commission

Let the agent know that the commission is flexible and is dependent on how quickly the property is sold. All of these should be put into writing. Prepare a budget and let them know how much they may lose, likewise you if the property isn't flipped at the appointed time.

Demand for References

You don't have to rely on only the things you are being told, you can demand the contact of those he has worked with earlier and confirm from them if it is wise to be involved with the agent.

Availability

It is important you get an agent who would always be available to take people to check out your property or who would be ready to take you with him to check out properties if you are the buyer. Ask them if they are involved in any other work asides being a broker. Make sure you deal with agents who work as full time because they tend to take their job more seriously than those who work per time.

Ask for Their Suggestions

Let the agent contribute his own quota of suggestion on things that work best for property sales. Savvy agents know what attracts buyers in an area they know the exact features the people in a particular location look out for in properties. They are in the best position to make these suggestions. Ask them if there are changes that need to be made to the house to increase its market value, good agents will always speak out because they will also feel the attractiveness of the house will make things easier for them too.

Personality

Chose an agent who is on the same page as you. When you are on a similar note, it is easier for you to sell out your property fast and at a favorable price. Agree on the price the house would be sold and how the house would be shown to potential buyers. It would be easier to work with someone you get along well with.

Even when you feel you had gotten yourself the best agent, make sure your property is placed on multiple listing services and think twice before signing an exclusivity agreement.

Getting a Realistic Property Valuation

Property valuation deals with the estimation of the value for a property which is mostly the market value. It is the process which governs the financial value of the real estate. It is restricted to work with fair market value, that is, the price at which an agent who knows the economic conditions wants to sell a property and the amount a buyer who also knows the economic condition is willing to buy it. Property valuation assumes each party understand the economic situation and are aware of the market value of the property and they are not forced to come to a compromise. Property valuation has four introductory support which includes demand, utility, scarcity, and transferability.

Demand is the degree of interest and the financial capability for purchasing property in the market. The utility is the capacity of the real estate to meet the needs and satisfy the use of the property by prospective purchasers. Scarcity, it can identify that there is not enough supply of real estate. Transferability explains how easy it is for real estate to be legally transferred from a person to a new owner.

Getting the realistic property value of the real estate is important for various reasons such as financing, property insurance, analysis of investment and tax payment. You can get a property's value through these appraisal methods:

- **Sales comparison approach:** It is an approach used to check the value of single-family homes. It is the estimation of value which is arrived at by comparing a property which was recently sold and has similar characteristics. Similar characteristics are called comparable. For properties to be comparable, they must be similar to one another, should less than a year difference and must have been sold under almost similar economic conditions. You also must take note of the size of the property, age and conditions of the buildings, location of the property and other physical features. Then, if all these conditions are met, the values can be compared, and the value can be leveled to be the same to estimate the market value.

- **Cost approach:** This method is used when selling properties that are not usually in the market or are only sold on rare occasions such as schools, government buildings, hospitals, and churches. It is used to know the value of the property that has been renovated or improved to contain one or more buildings. In this method, an estimate of value is made for each building and land, then the estimated are added to know the value of the whole improved property. The new value gotten would be the estimated value of the property. In the cost approach method, depreciation is put into consideration and the cost of fixing.

The methodology to use in calculating the cost approach is as follows:

1. Calculate the value of only the land using the sales comparison approach since lands do not depreciate
2. Calculate the costs of each building and the amount spent on improving it.
3. Calculate the amount of depreciation in the building and deduct the cost from the estimated construction cost.
4. Add the depreciation cost to the estimated value of the land and site improvement to determine the property value.

- **Income approach:** It is sometimes referred to as the income capitalization approach. This is the relationship between the amount of income an investor expects and the net income the property produces. It is used to calculate the value of properties producing income such as apartments, office buildings, shops and so on.

Exact property value is always demanded by the mortgage lender and it is also important to investors, buyers, and insurer. Appraisals are only performed by professionals.

Factors Affecting Property Valuation

There are factors that influence the value of a property; few of them are highlighted below:

1. **Location:** it is referred to as the highest factor that influences the market appraisal. Similar

properties will in a different environment have different prices. Some house cost more because they are in a more desirable environment. It may be due to the social amenities or closeness to public transportation, school or in some cases if the environment is serene and well secured. Some suburbs are abandoned and avoided by people due to bad roads or crime rates, therefore different postcodes bring about a difference in property value.

2. **Supply and demand:** The supply and demand for property determine its value. The market principles at a particular point in time determine the value the property will have at that time. Supply of property can be fixed at a particular time. To increase supply, more houses should be flipped, more properties should be built, or big properties are splatted. We do not have control over demand as we have an oversupply. Demand can change

relatively with time and it has a high capacity of influencing property value. When demand is higher at fixed supply, property value increases and house flippers will make use of the short-term increase to supply more and make huge profits. The demand for people can also be influenced by changes in the economy. When people make more money, they tend to think of getting more properties.

3. **Interest Rate:** When bank monetary policies are changed, this can have a positive or negative impact on property value. If banks increase interest rates and other loan givers also do the same, the average monthly mortgage repayment rises, and this affects that affordability of properties. So prices drop as there is competition, and everyone will just want to flip their properties even when they are at a loss. Likewise, when interest price reduces, property value increases.

4. **Population and demographics:** When people are looking for a way to live in a particular suburb, the demand for properties in that suburb increases. Also, the class of people living in a suburb determines the value of property in that environment.

5. **Economy:** Economic performance has a great effect on property value. If a country has a lot of employed people with great job opportunities, people will be able to afford expensive properties, and everyone will be benefited.

6. **Property size, facilities, and age:** The size refers to the area of land occupied including the compound and the size of the building. The bigger the landmass of the property, the higher its property value. Also, the older the house, the lesser the property value as the seller has done a lot of renovations coupled with up-to-date fittings. The presence or absence of facilities such as parking lots or

other important facilities is likely to affect the property value.

CHAPTER NINE

THE PROCESS OF PROPERTY FLIPPING

Property flipping is a step by step activity. Here are the steps that would lead you to successful flipping

1. **Create a business plan:** This is the step-in property flipping; you need to set a realistic goal, strategies and plan to make your flipping a successful one. Lenders will take you more seriously when you have a detailed business plan which is put into writing to serve as a guide to you. Your business plan should include your mission, goals and summary, financing options, lead generation plan, market analysis, sales plan and detailed internal procedures that can remind you of deadlines.

2. **Hire professionals to work with you:** You must find a team and the best choice you can make is to go for professionals. This makes your work faster as they are people who already know what is expected of them. In most cases, they are certain of cost and can even help to reduce cost by contacting the networks they know. Your team should include a good construction contractor, a realtor, an attorney, an accountant, and an agent. Making up a team that aids the rehabilitation and increase the pace of marketing is important for both short- and long-term success of flipping.

3. **Getting a property to flip:** There are various ways you can get properties to flip. You can hire a real estate agent that is familiar with the environment you are looking at. You can also contact a wholesaler who has a property of such at your desired location, you can also decide to check listings of properties for sale

online or in newspapers, this can be done either by paying or for free. There is also an option of you doing it manually which can be driving around neighborhoods to check if there are properties that can be of interest to you to be flipped.

4. **Buying a property:** When you have been able to locate a property that looks appealing to you, the next step is for you to buy it and begin working on it. You should always remember that your primary reason for buying the house is to make a profit and all other motives are irrelevant. No matter how god the condition of the house is, you must be profit-driven when bargaining for the property and don't buy a too-expensive house just because it looks good. Let your exit strategy be clear on your head and stick closely to your budget.

5. **Fix and flip:** The next thing expected of you after purchasing the property is to fix and flip immediately. During this, you don't have to hire people for everything, check for the things you can do by yourself and do them, sweep where necessary, break tiles, those works do not need expertise. Work with competent and honest contractors and be time conscious. Be available during the rehab, don't leave it without monitoring. Do decors that are generally appreciated and not too expensive. Drop your taste of a home aside and do what will look appealing to every sane man.

6. **Flipping the house:** Once you have finished the rehab and gotten to a point where the house is in good shape to be sold. It's your decision if you would work with a realtor to get the property sold or you will sell it yourself. Decide the type of realtor to be hired, the amount of money it would be sold,

the timeline for sale and how profitable is the project. What are the mistakes you made that shouldn't repeat itself in your next deal? Once the property is sold, the deal is closed.

Fixing or Straight Flipping

House flippers have options, you either decide to get a property, fix it and flip or you get a property at a cheap price and eventually sell it *without flipping*. The latter is referred to as wholesalers. The two options are aimed at the same thing, to make a profit. The most common form of flipping is the 'fix and flip'. The similarities among both are that they are profit-oriented, but they have clear differences and it later becomes your decision to choose the one that works best for you. The differences include:

- **Time management:** Although both of the options have to do with getting a property that would be flipped which consumes the same time but wholesaling is more time conscious because you sell off the property immediately you buy them and your market is larger because you have more people to sell to. You can decide to sell to house flippers or retails. While people involved in fix and flip must go through the process rehabbing and putting things in order to make the house attractive to a buyer, during this process, a lot of time would have been consumed.

- **Stress:** You don't have to go through the process of rehab when you settle for straight flipping, you don't need contractors as a wholesaler, all you are after is someone who would buy your property and you would get your profit. But in fix and flip, you must rehab the property, look for a competent contractor, supervise and do the few things you can to make them work faster.

- **The number of people:** Wholesalers do not require a lot of people, in fact, a team is a crowd in wholesaling. All that is required of them is to buy and sell but in fix and flip, you need a minimum of 5 professionals to get the best product.

- **Risk:** Fix and flip can only be done by people who are ready to take the risk. The risk of having to own a house for so long, the risk of a fix becoming a flop and so on. Wholesaling has less risk.

- **Marketing:** Marketing houses that are only flipped without being fixed is easier because you have varieties of buyer, even house fix and flippers can patronize you but for real estate investors who are involved in both fixing and flipping, you need all the marketing strategies you can ever think of because the circle of consumer is smaller.

Procuring a Proficient Plumber

If your property has a problem with pipes, then there is a need for you to include the hire of a plumber in your list. As you know that plumbing is a crucial work in a home, so you must be careful with your choice of plumbers. Don't tolerate bad plumbers, your property will look like a mess to buyers if the plumbing work is not neatly carried out. Here are the things to look out for before you allow the plumber to fix your pipes:

1. **Training and experience:** proper training and experience are important. Before you allow a plumber work on your property, make sure he is well trained in the field and has enough experience to handle plumbing issues. To be on a safe side, you can ask your friends for referrals or you search for online for reliable sources.

2. **Amount charged should be examined:** You have decided whether the plumber is charging fairly or not by making inquiries on how much he charges hourly. Remember you are into a business, so you should be calculative in your spending.

3. **Availability:** Make sure the plumber you are going for would always be available for emergencies and on time too. In this case, it is advisable you hire the ones that are close to you because if plumbing works are not attended to on time, it might cause great damage.

4. **Warranty:** The house is one that would be flipped, and it will not be a good market strategy for the house pipes to have issues in the first month of sale. Therefore, hire plumbers who are certain of the work they have done and gives you a warranty of not less than six months.

5. Insurance: make sure the plumber you hire is insured in case of an emergency to keep both of you safe. Do not hurry in the process instead, do proper research and get the best.

Getting an Excellent Electrician

Wiring a house is a complex system that requires great care from experts to be fixed. Amateurs should never be allowed to handle your property to avoid flops. Here are tips you can use to get a good electrician for your house flipping.

1. **Work with referrals:** The easiest step for you to get an electrician that would put your mind at rest is to talk with friends and neighbors to know if they have good and competent electricians that can work for you. This recommendation is very important.

2. **Permits or licenses:** Before you allow electricians work on your property request for their work permits and necessary licenses. An experienced and qualified electrician should have an issue with this request. Look for professional charisma and expertise when they explain how things can be fixed to you.

3. **References:** If the referrals didn't work, you can go online to search for companies that can help you sort this out. Then you can make your choice from there. When the person shows up, request to know if he came from the company with proof.

CHAPTER TEN

FINDING A BUYER

Prospective buyers and tenants begin their search for their next property online instead of the traditional way of getting in touch with a real estate agent. Buyers are, now more than ever, doing the Realtors legwork as they can access everything they need online, only involving the realtor when they have found something they like. This cuts down the time spent on apartment-hunting. Instead of going to see various listings in person, wasting precious time, the buyer can look at them online and pick whatever they like best then go see it in person. This is a time-saving endeavor.

That being said, there are millions upon millions of listings on the internet. Easily accessible to the prospective buyers that they may see someone else's and want to stick with that. The competition, in real estate, is cut-throat and you'll require competent marketing Techniques to get ahead and bring your business to the buyers first.

What we are going to focus on in this chapter is how to take your listings online and how to make it stand out.

1. Home Staging

This showcases the home decor possibilities of the apartment. It shows the potential of the apartment and it catches the eyes of the prospective buyer, who is surfing the net, faster and better than a sterile empty space. Home staging, apart from helping to speed up the buying or leasing process, it might also drive up the value of the listing with perception. This means that it looks good and the buyer that seeing it online would have a good perception of the value of the property based on what they have seen. Staged homes also have another Advantage over the upstaged home as it makes for excellent social media posting. Staged homes catch the eyes of the buyers both online and offline making your work easier

2. Eye-Catching Photography

The saying that "First impression matter" cannot be overstated in the world of real estate. A walk Street journal research found out that more than 90% of prospective buyers view the first photo of a real estate agent's listing (which is usually the outside of the property) for about 20 seconds before losing interest. This means that you have your work cut out for you. You must convince them to stay tuned and view the rest of your listing. Selling houses has to do with a lot of convincing and this starts online with pictures of your listing. Investing in quality photography would only help you tremendously and is a good move in staying ahead of the curve.

Also, another important thing to note with photography in mind is the best features of your listing. This would make your listing more photogenic and memorable. Remember, there are millions of listings online and we are trying to distract the buyers from the others long enough for them to settle on yours, so we have to put our best foot forward with eye-catching photography of the house itself as the cover photo of your listing and the best photos showcasing the best features of your listing in the best possible way. We hit them with amazing photos as soon as they sink their attention on the bait, that is, the first photo of your listing. This way, we strike while the iron is hot

3. Keywords

These are the things or advantages that your listing offers. Keywords are specially looked for by the buyer because it tells the buy what your listing has to offer.

There are two types of keywords; namely: The feature keywords and descriptive keywords. The feature keyword showcases the features that your listing boasts of, example;

- Proximity to public transportation
- Proximity to schools

- Walking distance to the park
- Skylights
- Amazing views

These feature keywords already tell prospective buyers what they are getting if they choose that piece of property.

Next is the descriptive keyword. These type aids in describing the listing in a manner that triggers the imagination of the buyer. Example;

- Spectacular
- Low maintenance
- Recently renovated
- New
- Marble floors
- Lots of space Etc.

Keywords that include the requirements of prospective buyers are very important to make your listing stand aside from the other. These might be feature keywords that show and tell the amenities and benefits that lie near the property or Imagination triggering descriptive keywords.

But, to do this, you must know what features or descriptions your buyers want versus the features the listings and the community offers. You need to know the neighborhood. The needs of various people in different stages of life differ exponentially and you must account for that.

All in all, you need to research what features the neighborhood boasts of versus the different types of people living in that neighborhood then you can use the information as the icing on the cake to sweeten the deal with the target audience. Domain.com.au and realestate.com.au. are demographic profile tools that can help you.

4. Social Media and Ads

The entirety of the world's opinion begins and ends on social media and this is where you need to be. You should have accounts on all the major social media players e.g.; Twitter, Facebook, Instagram, Google+, etc. You should use the accounts to promote your listings, to show then to the social media world. This way, your listings can reach a lot of people at once and if you catch a prospective buyer, you can be contacted as soon as possible.

Social media provides an avenue for you to reach out to millions of people at no special cost to you except your time. You can interact with other users, share your photos, etc., the possibilities are seemingly endless as the rewards would prove.

Prospective buyers would always want to show their family and friends the house pictures that they like through social media for second opinions. It would be a big advantage if you are already on the social media platform, armed and ready with photos to woo them.

Also, be ready to spend money on social media ads. With this, you can reach a lot of people bringing your business to their social media doorstep. As the saying goes "if Mohammed won't go to the mountain, the mountain would go to Mohammed", if the buyers won't come to your website, bring your website to them and shove it in their faces till they have no choice but to click through and find it decked out with beautifully staged rooms that show all the potential of the house and go through the keywords and house descriptions and title and they find everything they need in a house and they contact you and you reel them in.

The Crux of the matter is this, pushing your listings and your website on social media and with the added advantage of social media ads would help you get in touch with more people and would make referrals easier, especially on Twitter, where your account can be easily tagged and your pictures can be easily retweeted to person(s) interested in buying a property.

5. Virtual Reality Tour

Time is money. The less time you spend convincing a buyer, the more money you would make by attending to other buyers and the better you would be for it.

This is where a VR tour comes in. A virtual tour is a way of giving a tour of the house without giving a tour of the house. That means that the buyers watch a 3d virtual reality video of the house in a way that would showcase the house the way you would do it yourself. This gives the buyer as much understanding of the house as possible before they come down to see the property in person. The Advantages of the VR tour is that a lot of people get to see the listing without you being there in person to give them that tour. So anyone that comes to check it out in person and meet with you must have seen something they liked and all you need to do is throw on a little charm and the deal is closed. This cuts down the time-consuming effort of showing the house to everyone. Now, with a VR tour, that tediousness has been excised like a tumor and we have innovations audio-visual software to thank.

6. Local Sponsorships, Branding, and Contacts

It is vital to know that, if you want to be successful at finding buyers and selling houses, you need to start thinking of yourself as more than an individual realtor but as a brand that is made up of you and as it's common with brands, you get to pick a snazzy name, you get a logo and you carve a niche for yourself. You can decide to be that realtor that caters to the housing needs of the divorced or the newly Wed or the family Guy. Either way, you carve a niche of the market that is most profitable for you and you ride with it, not as a lone ranging individual realtor but as a brand that at a glance would convey the perception of professionalism.

Also, taking part in sponsoring events is a surefire way to get buyers attention. It is important to know that people rarely remember what they hear more than what they see. Sponsorship of events like local festivals, bake sales, sports teams, etc. is a sure way of getting your business out there because by Sponsoring these events, you get to Float your business brand on t-shirts, flyers, posters and so on. If your business is in their eyes and your name is in their mouths, you are going to be attracting buyers. Local sponsorship is a good way to advertise yourself and your brand by way of t-shirts, pens and other brand memorabilia.

Still on the topic of branding and how it would help you attract more buyers.

A brand needs a website, so you need a website. A website that is user-friendly with pictures of all your listings and with the necessary keywords to preach to the right audience. Your website should be easy to navigate and contain everything needed to decide on your website, like the features and pictures of said features of the neighborhood where your listings are in it. Your website should have your contact information clearly visible and accessible and you should be available to pick calls and answer questions at any time. You should have a creative business card, not a drab one that would end up getting tossed away. A business card that would leave a perception of who you are and what your brand is on the mind of whoever takes it.

Also, as a brand, you should get into partnership with other local businesses like restaurants. You can partner up with a local coffee shop and have your logo on their coffee mugs and napkins etc.

7. Locally Orientated

In real estate, it is important for your brand that you are locally orientated. This means that if anyone wants to get a new house or rent an apartment, you are the one they call. You need to get deeply saturated in the locality. Be the go-to person for meeting housing needs. Getting your brand a spot on the local newspapers is a good way of being in the localized spotlight. You don't want to sound too forward; you will want to come out as being professional in your field. You can write about issues that affect the town/city and the real estate market. Write about important issues in the town or the country at large and their effects on the real estate market. Use the newspaper column as an avenue to show off your acumen and come out as knowledgeable and informed not overly forward. You can also have feedbacks of people that have patronized your services published on your column. This is a way to convince more people to your trustworthiness. Trust is everything to people, no matter the business venture. People want to trust you and a great way of gaining that trust is through the testimonies of other people who trust you. Once you name or your brand name is associated with professionalism and trust, you are most certainly set.

8. Referrals and Call Tracking

After you close a deal, you don't want to close the relationship between you and the buyer. You don't know what possibilities lay in store for you, that's why it's in your best interest to stay in touch. Send them occasional movie tickets, holiday cards, birthday cards, occasional calls to check in on them and how they are enjoying the house. Stay fresh in their minds by staying not completely out of sight. Along the line, they may have a friend or a family member that needs a house or an apartment, if you are still in touch with them, they will refer you to him or her.

CHAPTER ELEVEN

COMPLETING THE SALE

1. NEGOTIATION

Negotiation is important in every business venture; scratch that, every life venture. We are always negotiating to get the best possible deals we want from whatever and with whoever we are involved in. As someone involved in the real estate business, you should not be afraid to negotiate or shy away from the negotiating table because you would be doing it a lot. In completing the sale of a house, after you have reeled in a prospective buyer, it's time to get down to brass tacks on the negotiation table. You must be smart and intelligent in order to negotiate from a place of strength to get the best deals possible. The smarter and more informed you are, the more likely you are of getting your way during negotiations.

Here are some tested and trusted negotiation techniques:

1. Escalation Clause

Including an escalation clause would bring you more offers and make your listing more competitive. Escalation clause would give your client, this is if you are selling someone else's house, or you if it's your house, multiple competitive offers. It is a great way to increase offers you get for a property thereby giving you or your client the best possible deal.

An example of an escalation clause goes like this; "we are therefore initiating an escalation clause. MR Henry has offered to pay $5,000 more than your highest offer".

An escalation clause turns the negotiating process into a low-key auction bidding war. It gives all the prospective buyers a heads up to up their ante if they want to secure the property, to the profit of your client.

2. The Different Types of Negotiation and When to Use Them

When negotiating, you can either go straight up for the best possible price you can get, or you can settle for a win-win fair price. In negotiations, it is critical to note the value dynamics. This refers to the things that are of less or no value to you but might be of high value to the other person. This is important in every sector of human endeavor where negotiations are being done and super important in real estate. Sellers are looking to previous house prices while buyers are looking to current house prices to figure out a comparatively fair price.

In real estate business, it is vital to know that, once you commit to a buyer, you can't legally accept offers from another buyer even at a higher price. This is what is called a "tight deal". So in a circumstance where you want to get the best possible deal you can, "a loose deal" in what is required. If you find a buyer and he/she makes an offer that is less than your estimate, you can get a little time reprieve to find a better offer and if you do, you can sell the house to the person with the better offer but a "breakup fee" would be required to end business dealings with the first buyer. The loose deal is poised to incorporate the various beliefs of the value of the property.

3. Take Your Job Seriously

You must take your job seriously to get yourself or your client the best deal possible. It is your fiduciary duty

4. Let Them Think They Are in Charge

Nobody likes to be told what to do, especially with their money. Nobody likes to be led especially when they feel they can do a better job by them. So, in real estate negotiating, you need to play to the buyers need to decide for themselves, to feel in charge of their choices.

A way to do this is to always give them the option of backing out of the deal with nothing lost except for time spent. Using phrases like "you may not agree but" is a proven way to get the buyer to agree to your suggestions. Skillfully downplaying your suggestions just enough to let the buyers mind wonder why you feel they would not want to do one thing or why they would refuse to do another. This would encourage them to do it, to make the decision you wanted all along but this time it would be of their own volition. We as humans are rebellious by nature. We want what people say we can't have it what they presume we are uninterested in. This would push us to do those things if only to prove people wrong. A skilled negotiator knows this and uses this to get as much headway in his negotiations as possible.

5. The Win-Win Negotiation Perspective

Negotiation isn't a battle of wills. There isn't always going to be a winner and a loser. Both parties can leave the table as winners. Negotiation is all about getting what you want by giving what you don't want. In the Real estate business, this refers to houses and properties. You are offering a house for sale and what you want is to sell it, the other person has money but needs to buy a house. You negotiate. You want to sell the house at a price that is perfect for you and your client, the buyer wants to buy that house at a price that is comfortable for him. You find where your interests intersect, the equilibrium, and you close the deal. Both parties leave the table with what they want. A win-win situation. Instead of facing the negotiation as a Calvary attack, you should learn to expect and provide the solutions that come out of the negotiation process.

Escrow

What is Escrow?

Opening an account with an escrow service is the First step in closing a real estate deals going forward after negotiation and as such, it should not be sidelined it overlooked. It is an exercise in caution as well as a deal closing facilitator. It facilitates transparency in dealings and encourages everyone to honor the deals made and hold their own ends of the bargain they have struck. The escrow account holds the documents and money and particulars involved in the deal and would act on it, whether to return it to the seller or pass it onward to the buyer at the conclusion of the deal, as instructed.

Escrow comes into play as an arrangement in which a neutral third-party acts as a middleman to hold documents and money to be used in a transaction to ensure that both parties are on their best behaviors. The third-party acts as a referee to ensure that everyone fulfills their obligations. It is the solution to dealing with people you don't trust. Most transactions aren't straight forward. Complications may arise on the way, the escrow provider is there to make sure that the deal is honored, regardless of complications. An escrow account is activated as soon as a signed agreement of the deal is delivered to the escrow service officer. The said officer would verify the contract, including inspections, disclosures, etc. are all completed.

Order Title Search

A title search is ordered by either the buyer or the seller for an in-depth examination into public records to check and ascertain the proper ownership and claims of a particular property. The search is to make sure that the property has a clean title for the purchase to go on. It is an evaluation process of the property.

A title company or a lawyer can be contracted to undertake this search and are expected to go through legal documents and records to accomplish their goal.

Although it is possible for the seller or the buyer to do this search on their own, it is not advisable because of the complexity of legal documents and the fact that the seller or buyer may not be qualified to undertake a title search.

This represents a safety measure in real estate dealings on the part of the buyer. The real estate agent or seller, that's you, can order the title search on behalf of the buyer. This is for a lot of reasons. Among them is;

- To protect the property or asset from anyone else that may come up to claim ownership of your property.

It is not entirely out of the realm of possibility that a seller would try to sell a property that doesn't belong to him or her. To quell any doubts and to move forward with the deal, a title search and examination should be ordered, and this is paid for by the buyer and as such, the buyer should be contacted before the title search and examination is being ordered.

An appraisal in real estate is a property/asset/land valuation process during which the value of the property is discovered. Real estate purchases and transactions require quality appraisals because not every house or property is the same. There are always mitigating factors and variables that offset the valuation of a property. For example, a studio apartment in Boston doesn't have the same value with a studio apartment in New York, even if they are the same shape, size, and even color. Other factors are considered during a home appraisal, as the location. Location is a vital variable in the appraisal equation but since a house cannot change its location, there are other factors that can affect the value of a property. Example:

Crime rate:

The higher the crime rate in a part of a town the lower the value of the house in that area becomes. This is because, no one wants to stay in a high crime environment and as people are trying to get out of that area, making it less desirable, the supply becomes higher than the demand which in turn reduces the value and cost of buying or renting properties in such areas.

Other factors that affect the value of the home includes upgrades and renovations done or to be done.

Appraisals are used as a platform for mortgage loans application, taxation, settling of estates on a will and to figure out a good sales price for a property.

An appraisal evaluates the permanent fixtures of the house and its surroundings. The appraisal doesn't take furniture or decor into consideration. Size, number, and state of rooms, location, and the overall condition of the house are what is looked for during an appraisal.

There is a common misconception about who sets the value of the property or who carries out the hone appraisal between the real estate agent and the home appraiser.

The difference is this. While both play crucial roles in real estate markets and frequently suffer role reversals and overlaps, they, often, come to separate conclusions on the issue of the value of a particular piece of property.

A real estate agent helps in the buying and selling of properties. Real estate agents may represent the buyer or the seller or may either the buyer or seller in any case. Real estate agents, most specifically listing agents, occasionally provide market estimates to their clients (the seller) of the value of the property. This estimate is to provide the seller with a sample of the nature and range of offers that he may come across during the sales process from the prospective buyers. Real estate agents take the mostly the same considerations that appraisers take in making their market estimates which includes, recent sales, and environmental demographic characteristics that may or may not attract prospective buyers.

An appraiser is a certified person that examines, closely, a piece of property or a house to safely determine its value. The appraiser does his examination in-person to successfully gather data to aid his examination. The appraiser studies market conditions, taking into consideration the comparable and variables in the calculation of the value of the property.

Sellers may be alright with the estimates of the agent, but buyers are often more satisfied with the ideas of both the agent and the appraiser, in order to get the best possible deal out of the purchase and not feel like they have over-spent.

In conclusion, although agents, especially professional and experienced ones can make valuable market Estimates

On a particular property, only a qualified appraiser can legally and officially make and perform an appraisal.

Home inspection

A home inspection is a non-intrusive examination of a piece of property whereby the condition of that property is determined. The home inspection is needed and is vital in the conclusion of a house sale. Qualified home inspectors carry out this task. During the home inspection, the inspector looks around and tries to correctly ascertain the conditions of the house at that moment in order to make a detailed report of the findings which would inform the client (the seller of the house or the buyer) about the state of their intended transaction. The home inspection doesn't include future projections if the state and conditions of the house. The inspection is all about now.

Just as the duty of home appraisals can be confused between the real estate agents and the home appraiser, the home inspection is often confused with a home appraisal.

A home inspection focuses on the conditions of the home, the conditions of the structure and the problems found in the home while the home appraisal focuses on the value of the structure.

It is important to not be overwhelmed by the prospect of buying a house that you forget to order a home inspection.

Home inspections save you from a lot of headaches and spending down the lane.

Reasons for home inspection include;

Knowledge and safety of the property:

After the home inspection, you are going to get a detailed report from the inspector on the state of the structure and the conditions of the interior. This would help you in deciding if you are still going to move forward with the purchase of the house or not.

It would inform the buyer of the repairs made or be made on the structure, the cost of maintenance needed for the property, etc. The home inspection gives the buyer a chance to back out of the deal if he/she finds the report unsatisfactory.

The report also highlights safety concerns like electrical systems that are faulty that could result in a house fire, faulty plumbing and other discrepancies that may exist in the house. The home inspection gives the buyer a chance to check out the risk and reward ratio of purchasing the house. Ultimately, requesting a home inspection is very important for the safety and security of the buyer, which is why it should not be forgotten or overlooked.

Information on the structural faults of the building is a major reason for a home inspection. Structural issues can be costly to fix and will require a lot of attention and time to remedy. A home inspection report gives the client a heads up on these things.

Negotiations

Home inspections influence negotiating because in-depth analysis and knowledge of the property would give the buyer leverage on the negotiation table especially when the home inspection report comes up with safety concerns and underlining structural issues and vice versa when the report shows no problems at all. Home inspections are therefore vital because of its effect on the outcome on real estate negotiations.

Budget Control

A detailed home inspection report gives the buyer a projection on the extra funds they will likely spend on repairs and maintenance if they go ahead with the purchase of the property. It helps the buyer evaluate his/her decision with projected expenses that would from the purchase with his/her budget boundaries in view.

Also, knowledge of the issues of the property will save the buyer from future costs if they back out of the deal. Home inspections give detailed information on the conditions of the house which would influence the buyer to make budget-wise decisions taking future expenses into consideration.

Maintenance

The professional home inspector report gives a projection on the maintenance and repair needs that the house needs and can also give quality advice on how to go about it. The home inspector has a wealth of knowledge and on the job experience that could and should be leveraged by the client to the maximum.

Sellers-Required Inspection

Some cities require the seller of a property to order a home inspection before putting the property up for sale. This is to ascertain the viability of the house and to ensure that a viable safety hazard isn't put on sale, in the first place, to unsuspecting buyers. This inspection, carried out by a home inspector, is what is called a sellers-required inspection.

The sellers-required inspection is the same as the buyer's inspection. The only difference is who the client is. The client, in this case, is the seller of the property. The sellers-required inspection shows the seller what may likely be found by the buyer's home inspection and can get whatever maintenance needed to be done before putting the building up for sale.

Having a home inspection done before putting the property up for sale would smoothen the negotiation process because the seller would be prepared for the buyer's home inspection and would have gotten the property for a smooth transition process.

Publicized Sellers inspection would do more for the sale of a house because it would reassure the prospective buyers about the state and conditions of the property, especially if the seller has fixed the property up and the maintenance report is publicized also.

Furthermore, the seller and/or agent have a duty to give candidate information about the state and condition of the piece of property that is listed for sale and a home inspection ordered by getting seller is the surest way for the seller to obtain such information.

A home inspection report is not compulsory on the to-do list that the seller must be all means undertake, unless the report lists important and non-negotiable issues that can tank your deal with a buyer, such as:

Structural defects such as roof leakage, crumbling floorboards, etc.

Safety hazards such as faulty electrical systems, basement flooding, wildlife infestation, etc.

Building code violations such as lack of smoke detectors etc.

These issues can break a real estate deal and make a buyer back out. A smart seller or agent would, after getting a pre-listing home inspection, fix up the necessaries and compulsories for a smooth business transaction.

Things That Home Inspection Covers

- Electricity
- Plumbing
- Vents and air conditioning
- Kitchen
- Floorboards
- Walls
- Heating
- The grounds around the property
- Basement
- Attic
- Lights (both the interior and exterior)
- Foundation (structural integrity)
- Preparing for the home inspection.

Paperwork: The seller would like to assemble the paperwork detailing the maintenance and renovations done on the house.

The seller can provide this to both the home inspector and the buyer. This aids transparency and will make the inspection go faster without a hitch.

Cleanliness: The home should be in tip-top shape. Decluttered and squeaky clean. Removal of objects that would impede the inspector of you think would not be right for a good first impression.

Utilities: The seller should endeavor to make sure that the utilities are connected and working properly because the inspector would check and if it isn't connected, the inspection would have to be rescheduled. This would put a wrinkle in the deal closing.

Signing Title and Escrow Documents

In preparation for closing the deal on the home, both parties would be expected to sign a fair number of documents to transfer the house from the seller to the buyer and to close the purchase. This would involve the signing of documents to authorize the transfer of payments from the escrow account to the seller and transfer of the property title to the buyer.

These documents will include:

The deed: this document, signed, would transfer the title of the property from the seller to the buyer. The law concerned property sales in a particular state would dictate the diction and form of the document. The deed is signed and declared public in the public records by the recorder of deeds in the county. This puts the buyer's name in the chain of title of the property so should in case the house needs to be sold and a title search is ordered, the county records would be available for verification of your title as the rightful property owner.

The bill of sale: this document, signed, transfers all the personal properties in the house to the new owner. Personal properties such as security installations, lights, furnaces, etc. This document would list the appliances or personal properties that are going to be transferred.

The seller's affidavit: This refers to a sworn statement confirming ownership by the seller of the property and listing all known defects or snags on the title of the property such as liens or pending situations that may cause a lien on the title of the property.

Tax declarations: A lot of states require the seller and buyer to sign declarations that disclose the purchase price of the property and such states also charge property taxes on the transfer of title and ownership of such properties based on the purchase price of the house.

Home Loan Documents: In the eventuality of a loan, the loan documents are prepped by the seller or the listing agent. The type of loan would determine the number of documents to be signed by the person loaned to.

The documents in a typical loan include:

The note: This shows the proof of your debt to the seller, the description of the terms of loan type and the avenues for debt transference and/or collection. The note would also state the amount of debt incurred the interest rates that apply and the deadline for payment. If the debt/loan is transferred or sold, the note will be handed over to whoever purchases the loan.

The mortgage: This is the agreement to offer up the property as collateral for the loan. This is also recorded in the county recorder records alongside with the deed. The mortgage means that although the house becomes the buyer's after the deal has been closed, if the buyer cannot pay the loan, the buyer risks losing ownership of the house. The lender of the loan is within his rights to foreclose the property in the event of non-compliance to terms.

Closing escrow: Closing escrow signifies the end of the transaction. The purchase is complete, and sale is done and dusted. Opening and closing of 'escrow' accounts are common to standard dealings in real estate as they symbolize the beginning and the end of the transaction. At the beginning of the transaction, the escrow account functions as independent and neutral third party, handling funds and important documents to be used during the transaction and negotiation to ensure fair trade until the end of the purchase, where the escrow account is closed and the documents and monetary funds are given to the respective persons. The seller sends all documents pertaining to the house to the escrow account service provider for safekeeping until the time when the buyer transfers the agreed sum of money for the property to the same escrow account agent. The agent then sends the money to the seller and the documents to the buyer, thus, concluding the transaction between both parties. As soon as this is done, the escrow is said to have done its duty and is therefore closed.

The closing agent of the escrow account takes care of all the important documents that are vital to the conclusion of sales. Documents that include; insurance invoice and receipts, receipts for initial opening deposits and closing payments, documents to register the mortgage and title deed of the property with the appropriate law courts. At the close of the transaction, the closing agent of the escrow account updates the deed of the house with the name of the new owner and hands over the document to the appropriate lending institution that the buyer is mortgaging the property on (this is in the case of the buyer applying for a mortgage loan to finance the purchase of the property). This is referred to as the recording process.

Mortgage fraud: This is the crime of material misinterpretation and misinformation of the required information needed to apply for a mortgage loan, in order to scam the lending institution into lending a higher sum of money than the collateral is worth.

Federal courts in the United States try mortgage fraud cases at the same level as bank fraud or money laundering with punishments that reach up to more than twenty-five years' incarceration. The rise of the level and occurrences of mortgage fraud has led many states to take the initiative to enforce their penalties on mortgage fraudsters to deter others from joining the ranks.

It should, however, be noted that mortgage fraud isn't the same as predatory lending. Mortgage fraud is carried out through with the aid of misinformation and disinformation on the part of the person that is applying for the loan. While predatory lending is done by agents of the lending institution or mortgage bank misleading the person or persons applying for the loan. Predatory lending involves the unethical, deceptive and unfair practices perpetrated by the agents of a lending institution to impose unfair and fraudulent loan terms on individuals.

The idea behind a mortgage fraud is obtaining more money from the lending institution with false information than would be possible if the information was true. A lie that influences the decisions of a lending institution to facilitate the approval of a loan application. Mortgage fraud is simply the falsification of information in order to obtain a loan.

There exist different kinds of mortgage frauds, namely;

Straw buying: this involves the use of loan applicants by the fraudulent individuals in order to obtain the loan and disguise the true transaction going on. The straw buyer would be in on the scam and would get paid off by the perpetrator.

Air Loans: This refers to mortgage loans taken by non-existent individuals with non-existent properties as collateral. This is only possible by the aid of loan appraisers and officers colluding to defraud the system.

Double Sales: This refers to the sale of the mortgage note of a property to multiple buyers.

A builder bailout: this is what happens when the owner and seller of the property give monetary incentives to the prospective buyer and the goes ahead to increase the purchase price of the house and gets an inflated value for the house from an appraiser causing the loan to be obtained by the buyer to be inflated.

Buy-and-Bail: This is a fraudulent scheme that is characterized by a homeowner on a mortgage with the value of the home fallen the amount owed to the lending institution. This homeowner applies for a purchase mortgage loan to get another house when this new property is secured; the homeowner allows the house to go into foreclosure while he/she is secured in the new home.

Foreclosure rescue fraud: this involves the proposal of help from foreclosure professionals, who promise to help the individuals in debt avoid the foreclosure of their property by the lending institution. The foreclosure experts collect money for services they can't render as the property will inevitably end up being foreclosed and the borrower would have lost a lot of money and their home.

Mortgage fraud isn't only restricted and perpetrated by individuals alone, large scale fraudulent activities carried out by businesses exist. The issue of mortgage fraud is a serious case, serious enough to have a separate

Department with separate operations in the Department of Justice and with the FBI that is solely dedicated to combating it.

There exist two reasons for mortgage fraud.

- Profit backed mortgage fraud
- Housing backed mortgage fraud

Profit Fraud: This is a common fraud type in which the perpetrators are the financial industry/sector insiders who use their in-depth knowledge of the intimate workings of the financial system to cheat both the mortgage bank and the individual applying for the loan out of a lot of money. Perpetrators include loan officers, corporate attorneys, mortgage brokerage officers, property and loan appraisers, etc. This type of mortgage fraud is possible by the collusion of these professional industry insiders to cheat the system for no other reason but to line their individual pockets. This type of fraud cases takes top priority with the Department of Justice.

Housing Fraud: This type of mortgage fraud is carried out with the acquisition of a property in mind of the borrower. The perpetrator falsifies his/her income information on the loan application form and then go ahead to bribe the appraiser to join in the fraudulent activity by falsifying the appraisal report and manipulate the value of the property.

Federal Laws

The principal federal law concerning house flipping is the 90-day rule and the 180-day rule.

This means that a property cannot be put up for sale if the property hasn't been occupied or hasn't been under the ownership of the seller for less than 90 days.

A house flipper is someone that buys a home, makes a few improvements and sells the home at an increased price to make a profit. The reason for federal laws regarding home flipping is that home flipping creates a rich avenue for possible mortgage fraud. Keeping in mind that house flipping is a legitimate business venture but when the value and prices of properties begin to skyrocket exponentially especially when little to no improvements have been made, this is the place and time that eyebrows get raised and the federal authorities have to step in with laws to govern and regulate the home flipping process and slow down those fraudulent cowboys.

This is the rationale behind the creation of the federal laws.

90-day ownership

180-day ownership

The 90-day ownership is the more restrictive if the two. The calculation of the 90-day period begins from the recording date of the transfer of the deed to the new owner, who is aiming at flipping the home.

The next vital date to be calculated is the signed contract agreement date and the federal housing authority case date.

These two documents must be signed and dated at least 91 days from the recording of the deed date for the sale to go through. If it isn't, the FHA will not authorize the loan the buyer may apply for in order to purchase the property.

The second time limit is the 180-day period. Under this time period, both the FHA case file date and the signed agreement date of the property must be 181 days after the transfer of deed recording date. This law is made to discourage mortgage fraud schemes that use straw buyers.

State Laws

The federal laws and regulations on house flipping apply in every state but some states have extra rules and regulations that help in the regulation of the real estate market as it pertains to house flipping. Most of these laws target disclosures that the seller must render before the sale can go through. It is important for anyone that wants to venture into the market of house flipping to check the state real estate property laws in order to avoid legal trouble.

CHAPTER 12

BENEFITS OF HOUSE FLIPPING

House flipping is a risky investment, and as with all business ventures, the higher the risk, the higher the rewards. The benefits of house flipping, if it is done legally, rest on the availability of buyers. Without people to buy the house that has been bought, renovated and inspected, the house cannot be successfully flipped. That being said, here are some benefits of house flipping.

Profit- The purpose that drives individuals into private business ventures is strictly profit. Individuals get into the business of flipping real estate to make more money than they already make and at a quicker rate. When done right, a real estate house flip can bring in thousands of dollars in a very short time and this is the biggest attraction of the house flipping business.

The major determinant in the making of profit in real estate flipping is knowledge. The more you know about the real estate flipping business the more money you can make from it. Experience is key.

Real estate flipping can further an individual's education on matters of real estate. A real estate house flipper may start off as having little to no understanding of the workings of the real estate dealings but the longer he/she stays on, the more first-hand experience the person gets. Especially in getting quality appraisals, home inspections, negotiations and other important disclosures that a seller and buyer needs to know to smoothen the property purchase ride. Also, time spent remodeling, upgrading and on renovations of the property, if the flipper does them himself, would give the individual quality insights into the world of building construction. The individual gains insight into the cost of building materials, and home maintenance, how to attend to small I in the structural integrity of the house before it becomes a big issue.

A home flipper also gets on the job experience on how to go about the sale of the property. Learning what exactly the people want and how to tailor the renovations to meet their desires. This is possible by quality research into the preferences of the homeowners and potential homebuyers in an area. This way you can get to know what your buyer wants and demands, and you can plan to meet their needs with your supply.

Experienced house flippers always budget for delays that can't be calculated into the home-flipping equation. Things like delays in construction, delivery if building materials and building permits, and the cost of holding on to the house in the absence of buyers.

The first-hand knowledge gained by house flipping helps in the profit-making endeavor.

Satisfaction

House flipping can be self-rewarding apart from the profit-making aspects. When a person buys a rundown crappy property and renovates it, the person creates a model home out of barely anything. Having a vision and creating that vision of an ideal home is personal pride and is a source of satisfaction along with the profit made on selling the house. Renovation of a rundown home can be a relaxing and rewarding experience. You are building something beautiful out of almost nothing and selling it to people who would be happy to enjoy what you have built. You are going to be putting smiles on the faces of families. This is a form of satisfaction that keeps some house flippers going.

Self-employment

One of the great benefits of flipping homes is that you are your own boss. This means that you do answer to only yourself and the federal and state laws regulating house flipping, but mostly yourself. As your own boss, you set your own time, you make your own decisions and all that.

This might be a sweet candy gone sour if you lack the discipline and determination needed to be good at your job and make as much profit as possible without going into fraudulent activities. Because you are on your own, you oversee all the executive decisions you make, in charge of budgeting because it's your money, in charge of making sure everything is updated and ready at the time of sales. There is no safety net. The pay(profit) depends on the work. Bad decisions lead to bankruptcy. Home flipping gives the average man the opportunity to be his own man and eat the fruits of his labor. Be they sweet or sour. While this means that the person puts in a lot of work, it means that the profit belongs to the person since he/she is self-employed and not working to make someone else rich.

Risks Involved

There isn't enough sugar in the world to sugar coat this. House flipping is a very tedious and stressful business that can become extremely time-consuming. You can hardly be prepared enough. There will always be something to test your patience, resolve and determination.

Things will take longer than expected to come through. Mistakes will be made. Your temper will be lost, found and lost again. The longer you hold the property, the more bills you pay. Everywhere you look there is something to be done. You seem to have a lot to do and so little time. You may get confused and turned around a lot during the process especially if it's your first time. It is a very stressful procedure with pitfalls lurking beneath every bad decision. The only way to avoid stress is with experience and the only way to gain experience is by starting. Do you see where this is going?

Here are some of the risks and obstacles to flipping houses.

Losing Money: It is very possible for a house that you want to flip ends up as a flop. Losing money that you can't afford to when the market doesn't allow for the house to be flipped. You either don't get anyone that wants to buy the house or extracurricular expenses like building materials being more expensive than expected, contractors delaying the project making you hold on to the property longer than you planned for, come out of nowhere to rob you blind.

Taxes: After the renovations are done, the city officials may likely increase the rate on your property tax of the house, because the value of the property has gone up. This will affect your financial situation because though the value has gone up, you haven't sold the house yet and as such your finances are still the same if not drastically reduced due to the cost of buying and renovation of the property and you may have to pay the tax yourself.

The higher tax on the property may turn buyers away who would likely be scared if the high tax bill on the property.

Also, another scary thing is that you can also lose a lot of your profit to the IRS. Any profit made on property investment is subjected to taxation Called the capital gains tax. Your capital gains tax bill will vary, depending on how long the property stayed under your ownership, between under or above a year. There is always the option of postponing payment of the tax bill to a future date, but this might not be advisable because you might make less money later and won't be able to pay up or you might just plain up forget. Either way, you may be charged with tax evasion, which is a serious offense.

Holding Costs: If the property is still yours, you will have to pay the mortgage (if the property was mortgaged), taxes, and property maintenance.

Maintenance such as snow plowing, grass cutting, etc. All to make sure that it's in tip-top shape. The longer you hold the property, when you aim to sell it, the longer the miscellaneous costs pill up till you are buried in bills. You lose money the longer the building stays in your possession. The longer the property stays for sale, the lower the price. This is because the seller might already be fed up with the building and would want to offload it on the first buyer that comes his/her way. Desperation would force the seller to reduce the price of the property to please the buyer. This would eat into any profit that was projected at the beginning of the flip.

Stress: Real estate dealings are always stress-inducing, even more so, house flipping. From locating the property to buying the property, then fixing it up, dealing with city officials, inspections, appraisals, finding a buyer, convincing the buyer. The stress is always beside you like a second shadow or a faithful dog.

Potential Tax Consequences of House Flipping

Ignorant and inexperienced real estate flippers forget to plan for the tax consequences of their flipping transactions, but the IRS doesn't forget. Flipping houses is typically not calculated as passively investing by the IRS. The IRS regards house-flipping as an active income generation investment and as such it must be taxed accordingly. Active income (profits) from flipped properties are taxed on rates from as low as 10% to as high as 37%, especially when the resale of the property Happens before the property lasts more than a year with the flipper.

To the IRS, the real estate flipping occurs as a dealer (house flipper) buys properties and resells the property to buyers as the normal course of trade and as such, the income of the dealer would be considered and taxed as an ordinary income. Investors in real estate that hold properties short term and resell them occasionally are also considered dealers and are taxed accordingly.

On the other hand, income generation made possible from the sale of properties held by the seller for longer than one year is subjected to the capital gain tax rate (long term), with a tax rate of between 0-20%. An investor can decide to hold on to the property in order to qualify for this tax bracket and pay less tax when the house is finally sold

House-flipping is governed by complicated tax rules. Here are some of them:

1. Investor or Dealer-Trader:

The tax treatment and consideration the IRS gives to a flipped property is determined by how the flipper is viewed. Is he/she an investor or is he/she a full-time Dealer-Trader? Although, there is no official yardstick for the differentiation of who investors and the flipping professionals.

The IRS tries its best to determine which category the tax subject belongs and taxes accordingly.

2. Capital Gains Tax:

The profit that is generated by the sale of the property is called a capital gain. The tax levied on this profit is called the capital gains tax.

The amount of money paid as tax varies accordingly with the duration the property spent under the ownership of the seller. The sale of the property owner for a short time (a year or less) sets a short-term capital gain tax in motion. This is kind of capital gains tax is levied at the normal income rate. If the ownership of the property is for longer than a year then the sale qualifies for the long-term capital gains tax, which currently stands at 15-20% or the profit.

Investors can bring down and offset the tax rate if they get to sell a high profit-making house in the same year that they sold a property with a long-term capital gain tax on the profit, especially if they made a loss on it.

The profit and the loss would offset each other allowing the investor to break even.

3. Rollover Provisions:

A lot of house flippers imagine the deterrence of their taxes by selling a property and promptly investing it in another property. While this is possible in some cases and to specific people. This is available to only investors in real estate not to the dealer- traders.

4. Active or Passive Income

The generated income and profit of dealer-traders from flipping is referred to as an active income and as such, it is subjected to the normal tax rates along with a 15% tax for self-employment. There seems to be a lot of taxes that really affect Dealer-Traders. Moving on. The tax treatment and consideration of the profit generated through rentals us different.

Income from rent is referred to as passive income and it is taxed differently.

A major benefit that Dealer-Traders enjoy is the deduction of losses in full in the year of the sale, whereas investors are limited to the deduction of the number of losses they recognize on real estate dealings in a year.

5. Corporation versus LLC

Incorporating your private home flipping business means separating the business activities from your personal life and reduce and Private liability for the profit or losses accrued in the business. But on the downside, this doesn't change your tax bills or the tax status. If anything, it would be a beacon to announce to the IRS that you are a Dealer-Trader.

6. Deductible Expenses

Professional house flippers get to write off many business expenses. For example, funds spent in purchase and upgrade of a property is referred to as a capital expenditure. This is because the expenses were made with the capital of the home flipper. The capital expenditure can be deducted from the profit (taxable income) after the sale of the home. Other deductibles include office expenses, regardless of if the person works from his/her apartment (home office) or a real office. Other business expenses such as phone calls, rent, making and printing of business cards, utilities, just to name a few are fully deductible.

House flippers that use their cars for transportation for business can also put up travel expenses for deduction as a capital expenditure. The IRS calculates this in two ways. The first is called the standard mileage tax rate.

This is the calculation if the miles traveled for business multiplied by the standard rate which is 54cents per mile.

The second way involves the deduction of actual vehicular expenses which includes oil, fuel, and other maintenance done on the vehicle. To make this type of claim, the person would need to make and maintain an accurate logbook that would track mileage and Keep receipts that indicate repairs and fuel purchase for easy evaluation.

This means that anything that constitutes or can be classified under capital expenditure is deductible from the profit before taxation.

A major tax discomfort that afflicts dealers is that the tax consequence of flipping a house can range between 25.3% and 52.3%. This largely depends on the tax bracket of the dealer but to say the least, the dealer (house flipper) should not count his chicks just yet because the IRS is the gift that keeps on taking.

If you are lucky enough and the IRS doesn't slap the "dealer" name tag on you and you go in generating your income from flipping properties and selling them either below or above (but most especially above) the one year mark, you will be eligible to be taxed at the capital gains tax rate. The long-term capital gains tax rate is lower than the short term (which is the same rare as the ordinary income tax without the extra self-employment taxes that dealers Pay) but the both are lower than the tax rate imposed on dealers.

Though this rarely happens, as the IRS is always thorough, but it still happens. So for anyone that reads this and decides to give the real estate flipping business a try, you might just be one of the lucky ones.

Furthermore, a myriad of miscellaneous expenditures can be added to the deductibles like costs for obtaining building permits, legal fees, accounting fees.

The easiest way to keep track of possible deductibles is setting up of separate accounts for each property making the tax process easier and avoiding confusion that may likely give birth to terrible tax problems.

Also, due to the confusing tax laws that regulate real estate dealings, a house flipping business venture that is just starting out would be wise to recruit experienced accountants that are familiar with the real estate business and laws. This would be a positive step in ensuring smooth sailing in the turbulent storms of house flipping.

CHAPTER THIRTEEN
THE BUSINESS PLAN

Deciding to begin investments in real estate holdings must be preceded, backed, and supported by a viable and well thought out business plan, due to the amount of money and high risks involved.

This strategy or business plan should be made on the foundation of in-depth analysis and research of the target market, the financial quandaries and risks inherent in undergoing this investment.

The first decision to make is deciding whether you will fix and flip or you will buy and hold.

In this chapter, we will be looking at the pros and cons of buying and holding as an alternative to fixing and flipping but we will run through some pros and cons of fixing and flipping.

1.Fix and flip:

As we know by now and as it has been discussed in this book in the above chapters, the fix-flip strategy involves the purchase of a property that is acquired under the market value, renovation of said property and resale of the piece of property to make a tidy profit all in a short time.

Successful and profitable fix-flipping requires good negotiations and speed. The faster the house or property is flipped, the less holding costs, that can cripple the unsuspecting, is paid by the seller, the more time that would be spent getting on with the search for other houses to flip.

Advantages:

The first pro on the list is the quick profit realized by the dealers. The quickly generated profits have a major enticing quality that pulls more people to this strategy. The fix and flip strategy put more capital in the pocket of the dealer for more investment.

Also, the market is marginally easy to navigate and predict, which would permit the dealer to draw up close to perfect profit and loss projections for his /her investments.

The capital isn't at risk for as long a time as with the buy and holds strategy.

The rewards of the risk taken with the capital come quickly which frees the investor to invest more and flip more.

Flipping generally requires less time from incubation to fruition.

Getting the Flip worthy Property

Properties that are intended to be flipped are always gotten at below the market value. This is due to the acquisition, renovation and resale cost involved, not to mention the prospect of not finding a suitable buyer and the seller having to hold on to the house that he/she doesn't want while holding costs pill up. So what does the smart dealer look for?

Repossessed properties: properties like these are financial distress and nuisance to the owners. Investors/dealers must have credible real estate market knowledge and good networking skills to swiftly acquire these kinds of properties with minimal expenses.

2. Fixer-upper:

Properties in this category are in a dire need of repair. These properties need severe structural reintegration and design upgrade for them to be back on the market. Fixer-uppers are purchased by an investor way under the market value and if the investor has what it takes to meet the repair challenges that the property poses, then, a cool profit can be made. The house can also undergo massive remodeling that can make it appealing to suit a specific market.

Disadvantages:

Expenses that weren't planned for such as obstacles in the remodeling, overspending, scarcity of buyers can make the investor to hemorrhage money instead of making money.

Repossessed properties get purchased in a way that the investor may overlook and misjudge and miscalculate on the core issues that may plague the property.

Flipping properties can become a hell of taxes and financial mismanagement problems for the dealer. Best case scenario, you make no profit and barely break even. Holding costs eat into the budget and drown the investor in mortgage bills, insurance bills, and other mundane expenses. Worst case, IRS takes everything.

Flipping properties is stress-inducing as it entails the coordination of construction and renovation crews to meet up with deadlines.

Enough of the fix and flip, let's move on to the buy and hold strategy.

If you are searching for relatively safe avenues for increasing your income and cash flow, then the buy and hold real estate investment is just the thing.

Investors into real estate often, begin investments for the purpose of greater freedom in their finances. This is possible with the slow but steady cashflow of the buy and hold real estate strategy. The popularity of the real estate market is on the rise as people from different walks of life are investing in real estate. This is a great time to invest in real estate and have a piece of the positive cash flowing in the real estate market. This cash flow is basically the leftover funds that remain after all the mandatory financial regulations have been met. This is your profit.

The buy and hold strategy is straightforward. You purchase a property with the intention of fixing it up and holding onto it for a long time while the value appreciates and, in the meantime, you rent it out to tenants that meet the criteria.

Reasons behind Buy and Hold Strategy

Equity

If the investor bought the property on a loan then, as soon as the investor begins to make reparations to the lending institution from the rent collected, the investor is building equity with the property which can be leveraged for the purchasing other properties.

Cash Flow

$500 - $1000 per month may not seem all that positive but collecting $500 every month from five properties is a different story. Building your portfolio would build up your cash flow. Which can be, in turn, reinvested into the business or diversified?

Tax Benefits

Ownership of rental properties has the advantage of deduction in mortgage insurance premium, reduction of property tax, among other things.

Wealth growth is possible and feasible by the application of the 1031 exchange advantages that help curb tax burdens that would dam the cashflow.

Appreciation

Buying real estate to hold has both long term advantages and short-term advantages. The major short-term advantage is the rent collected from the tenants. This keeps the property up and running for when the time for resale nears.

The long-term benefit is the tidy profit that would be made on the resale by the appreciation of the property.

The goal of the buy and hold strategy is to buy a property, hold it long enough for the value to appreciate enough, then reselling it for a huge profit.

Resale Profits

Even though the outcome of the sale of the property depends on the real estate market conditions as at the time the building is listed for sale.

You can successfully put the property for sale at a time when the value of the property has increased thereby making a tidy profit from it.

Rent

At the onset of inflation, you can always raise the rent of your property accordingly if the market can bear it. Since inflation isn't guaranteed and since no one really wants to experience it, we shouldn't dwell on that. Nevertheless, if you can safely increase the rent on your properties then that would increase your cash flow.

Real estate investors that invest in the buy and hold strategy should be able and must be prepared to wait and hold on throughout the buy and hold process, especially the holding process.

The ultimate end of the buy and hold process is the sale of the property.

The buy and hold process is like eating cookies (rent) while the main meal is still cooking (end sale). The waiting process may get tedious and the investor may want to just give up and sell but this is where patience as the strong suit comes in to save the day.

The investor must be patient to sell at the perfect time to reap major benefits. An experienced real estate agent may be hired to give advice and counsel on when this appointed time is and to facilitate the sale of the house.

The buy and hold real estate strategy is all about the purchase of a property and holding on to it for a long time by putting it up for rent while waiting for the value of the property to mature and improve before selling.

Though this strategy has its risks, it is regarded as a simple and safe way of real estate investment.

The dealer/investor income is generated through monthly rent collected from the tenants occupying the property. The holding costs of the property are covered by the tenants.

The qualities needed and required for a profitable buy and hold operation is LOCATION. This involves buying properties in places where people want to live. Where you would easily find tenants. The longer the property stats empty, the less profitable the future of the investment looks. Investors that aim to buy and hold are also on the lookout for properties in areas that the value of a landed property is projected to rise in a decade or more. The buy and hold investor plays the long game.

Properties like duplexes and the like make valuable and profitable buy and hold acquisitions because they can serve as a way of Passive income generation or as a residence for the investor.

Advantages

The passive strategy (buy and hold) is a time-proven and reliably safe way, if not the safest way, of real estate investment that appeals to first time and seasoned buyers of real estate.

Buy and hold strategy causes less stress and problems because the investor has already made plans to keep the property for a long time and has rented the property to raise revenue to handle the holding costs that will accrue. The investor is not running against a clock to meet with a deadline. He/she is relaxed and unstressed. Also, the longer the property stays with the investor, the lower the property tax rate paid. Long term increase in property value and profit-making is easier to plot than short term increases.

Disadvantages

Rental properties also come with logistical and legal problems that arise from mismanagement.

Vacancy levels will be subject to external conditions beyond the control and capacity of the investor.

Locating individuals who would be quality long-term tenants might become a chore.

Below are some important questions that an investor should ask him/herself when deciding if they should fix and flip or buy and hold.

- When do you need your capital back?
- How soon are the property prices and value expected to reduce?
- Do you have enough funds to purchase, renovate and resale a property?
- How good is your networking skills the necessary sectors that play limited roles in real estate dealings?

- How comfortable are you with real estate dealings that are high risk?
- Are you prepared to pay more taxes?

The answer to the question of the best investment in real estate is best left for the individual or group of individuals that decide to invest in real estate.

The investor needs to ask himself/herself why he/she needs to invest in real estate and if the risks are worth the rewards.

There are several reasons why individuals invest in real estate. Real estate market is more understandable that the stock market. It is easier to plot and project your future profits and losses from a careful study of the market and its influences.

The real estate market aids during inflation periods because of the rental rates on properties increases in lockstep with inflation prices, thereby keeping the cash flow flowing.

The real estate market is a source of capital especially during the times when the stock market decides to nosedive. Equity generated from real estate dealings and investments provides capital for financing other business enterprises.

Your decision on whether you should buy and hold or buy-fix and flip depends on truthfully and honestly answering these questions above along with the situation of the prospective investor's finances.

Individuals or groups of individuals that wish to make real estate investment as a primary source of income should probably consider fix and flipping. But, in the long run, and the long term, the buy and hold strategy is the safest strategy available for real estate investments.

Conclusion

This aim of this book is the enlightenment of would-be investors on the pitfalls and high points of property investment, house flipping, and ultimately buying and holding properties as an alternative to flipping.

This book is also for those already involved in real estate at one level or others who need to know more about the real estate market. This book has you covered.

The residential: which covers properties used for residential purposes?

The commercial: This type refers to the pieces of properties that are used for commercial purposes.

The Industrial: this covers the warehouses and factories and research facilities. The History of house flipping was also talked about. To understand how far real estate investments have come, you will need to go back to the beginning. Beginnings that extends to before the revolutionary war.

The enactment of rights to ownership of property marked the single most important moment in real estate investment, growth, and development. Though as covered in the book in the first chapter, the real estate industry may be as old as man himself. The prospect of reaping enormous profit from property sales was and still is the propellant of the engine if real estate investment. It would suffice to say that ambition brought the real estate business to where it is today that the construction, purchase, and resale of real estate have become a common income generation scheme.

There exist a lot of technical support tools that would be very useful to the real estate property flipper that would aid in his/her business adventures.

These include:

House canary: which is an online platform that analyzes data to aid investors by showing and computing the true value of a property that is being cased? This online app caters to the newbies and to the professionals.

DealMachine: This app helps in the facilitation of opportunities to purchase properties.

Property fixer: This is a must-have technical tool for every property flipper.

Magic plan: This software helps in the estimation of the cost of flipping properties through a sophisticated but simple 3d augmented reality output.

Patch of land: This is an online application that connects the flipper to lending institutions that can finance the flipping.

All these apps are great additions and helpful tools for the real estate house flipper.

There are also options for financing the acquisition, repairs, and resale process. You can either finance the operation by yourself or apply for loans to facilitate the flipping.

The next thing after securing funds for the transaction is finding the property to be flipped.

This begins with finding the right neighborhood, check market housing statistics; confirm the condition of the property, budget forecast and calculation projected profit from flipping. After finding the property, you (the buyer in this case) should get a good agent to help with the purchase.

A good real estate agent would help in understanding the workings of the purchase process, credible property evaluation and you will get to know the different factors that affect real estate such as the neighborhood, the location of the neighborhood and the community. Understanding these factors that influence property value is very important. Even though as a property investor using the fix and flip strategy you would most likely be purchasing properties at below the market value, this information would aid in the planning of the re-sale of the flipped property.

The real estate agent would also assist in Assessing and projection of the profit-making ability of the investments. This book also enumerated and explained the processes involved in house flipping.

Though it is possible to make a lot of money flipping houses the process can get tedious especially for newbies but lucky for you, this book is here to help with the steps that include:

- Quality Research on real estate dealings, markets, and management
- Budgeting and business strategy formulation. It is important to plan your finances beforehand. Ask yourself if you have the money, personally to finance your investment or if you would take a loan. Either way is fine, but you need to make a viable business

plan that would contain all the plans and projections (profit or loss) of the investment

- Be prepared for miscellaneous and unaccounted costs.

- Find the property to be flipped

- Purchase the property with all the necessary documentation

- Renovate and try to adhere to your deadlines to avoid hemorrhaging money through holding costs.

- During, or better yet, before you purchase the property you Should already have good and competent plumbers, building contractors and electricians that would deliver promptly with quality repairs to the property for a smooth fix-flip process. The speed of the renovations greatly affects how soon the house can be resold since the house cannot be flipped if it hasn't been fixed. That defeats the entire fix-flip process.

After doing all the above, you get the home appraised and inspected to ensure that you are not in violations of any laws there is no asbestos in the home.

- The structural integrity of the property is firm.
- Molds and termite infestations
- The basic utilities like Central heating and central air conditioning are in tip-top shape.
- No leaky roof.
- Absence of lead-based paint on the walls
- The floorboards are not loose.
- The plumbing is working.

To name just a few things.

After the appraisal, to discover the value of the property and the home inspection, that is to find out how safe the property is. Then it is time to get a buyer

The sooner you locate a new buyer and you proceed in the resale of the property, the sooner you get to rake in your tidy profits.

Though this seems easy in theory, it can get difficult and you should be ready for that.

Finding a buyer is difficult if you don't know how to go about it. This is another good reason why this book was written, in the first place. To keep would-be investors and house-flippers in the know on how to go about tricky real estate dealings as it pertains to property flipping and so on.

Prospective buyers and tenants begin their search for their next property online instead of the traditional way of getting in touch with a real estate agent. Buyers are, now more than ever, doing the Realtors legwork as they can access everything they need online, involving the realtor when they have found something they like. This cuts down the time spent on apartment-hunting. Instead of going to see various listings in person, wasting precious time, the buyer can look at them online and pick whatever they like best then go see it in person. This is a time-saving endeavor.

There are millions upon millions of listings on the internet. Easily accessible to the prospective buyers that they may see someone else's and want to stick with that. The competition, in real estate, is cut-throat and you'll require competent marketing Techniques to get ahead and bring your business to the buyers first.

What we are going to focus on in this chapter is how to take your listings online and how to make it stand out.

Home Staging: This involves eye-catching staging of the home to highlight its potential to the buyer.

Quality Photography: As more and more properties are listed online; you would need something additional to make your own listings stand out and quality photography is the way to go.

Keywords: This factor in, when you are making the property descriptions. Research into the neighborhood and your target audience would let you find out the specific things the buyers that you are targeting needs. This is called keywords. There are two kinds of keywords as stated in the earlier chapter.

Social Media Ads: Ads on social media platforms greatly affects the rate at which you find buyers. With the millions of people on different social media platforms, it would be a lapse of due diligence for you to not use these platforms to advertise your property.

Virtual reality Walk-in: This grants the potential buyer a way to get shown around the house without the seller being present. This is an awesome tool that speeds up home hunting.

Other ways include call tracking, local orientation, and local sponsorship and branding. For more information, you could go back to chapter nine.

After you have found the buyer, it is time to bring him or her down to the negotiation table and there are tested and trusted ways of how to get this done effectively.

Inclusion of escalation clauses would help in getting you the best deal. An escalation clause declares to the buyer, the presence of another buyer that is ready to pay more for the same property. This makes the sales process to evolve into an auction but with extra steps and less gavel-banging.

It's also vital to know what you want from the deal and negotiate accordingly. Do you want to get the maximum price, or do you want to initiate a win-win situation? Discover which deal you desire and negotiate with that in mind.

It is important to always take the negotiation seriously as it is your job. If you are a private investor who flips properties to increase his financial freedom or if you are a realtor, working with an agent, you still have to take the job seriously and professionally.

Also, you should make the buyer feel at home and in charge of the negotiation. This would make him/her feel at ease and may end up doing what you want.

Finally, the winning perspective. You should enter the Negotiations with a mindset that you are going to walk out of there with a win. If you are already defeated on your head, it would affect your attitude during negotiations. Also, negotiation isn't a warzone and should not be treated as such. This is very vital in getting your way and not scaring the buyer away.

Other information you need to begin and complete a real estate deal includes:

Opening of an escrow account: This is a third party that takes care of the funds and documents involved in the transaction in order to ensure that both parties are on their best behavior.

Title search: this is a search that is ordered by the buyer or the seller to confirm the owner of the property to prevent any unfortunate future quandaries. The title search can be carried out by an attorney or a title search company.

Buyer's appraisal: This is an appraisal initiated by the buyer to find out the value of the home about to be bought.

Home inspections: This is carried out by a professional home inspector to make sure the property is safe and up to standard for habitation.

Disclosures: There are federal and state mandatory laws on what must be disclosed by the seller to the buyer before a real estate transaction is completed. Disclosures vary from state to state, so the Flipper should be informed about the mandatory disclosures in the state.

Closing escrow: After the deal has been finalized, the buyer sends the money for the house to the escrow account, then the escrow account agent transfers the money to the seller and the signed title documents and deeds of the property to the buyer.

Thus, the real estate transaction is concluded, and the escrow account is closed. Real estate dealings begin with the opening of an escrow account and end with the closing of the escrow account.

There are mortgage loans that are available for the use of the buyer to purchase a property but there are also mortgage fraudsters that use the mortgage loan system to cheat the banking system.

This is a crime of material misinterpretation and misinformation of the required information needed to apply for a mortgage loan, in order to scam the lending institution into lending a higher sum of money than the collateral is worth. There are several laws put in place to combat mortgage fraud, both federal and state laws.

There are different types of mortgage frauds listed in the book and they are;

Straw buying: This involves the use of loan applicants by the fraudulent individuals in order to obtain the loan and disguise the true transaction going on.

Air Loans: This involves an application for mortgage loans taken by non-existent individuals with non-existent properties as collateral.

Double Sales: This refers to the sale of the mortgage note of a property to multiple buyers.

Builder bailouts

Buy-and-bail

Foreclosure rescue fraud

Mortgage fraud isn't only restricted and perpetrated by individuals alone, large scale fraudulent activities carried out by businesses exist. The issue of mortgage fraud is a serious case, serious enough to have a separate

Department with the federal authorities solely dedicated to it.

The two reasons behind mortgage fraud stem from profit-making and home purchase. This is gone over at length in chapter 11 of this book.

House flipping is a risky investment. But as with all business adventures, the higher the risk, the higher the rewards. The benefits of house flipping, if it is done legally and properly outweighs the risks. Although the benefits generally rest on the buyers. Without people to buy the house that has been bought, renovated and inspected, the house cannot be successfully flipped.

This can't be overstated. House flipping is a very tedious and stressful business that can become extremely time-consuming. You can hardly be prepared enough. There will always be something to test your patience, resolve and determination.

Risk 1:

Taxes:

After the renovations are done, the IRS officials would likely increase the rate on your property tax of the house, because the value of the property has increased. This will affect your financial situation because though the value has gone up, you haven't sold the house yet and as such your finances are still the same if not drastically reduced due to the cost of buying and renovation of the property and you may have to pay the tax yourself.

Risk 2:

Stress: real estate dealings are always stress-inducing, even more so, house flipping. From locating the property to buying the property, then fixing it up, dealing with city officials, inspections, appraisals, finding a buyer, convincing the buyer. The entire coordination process is a super stressful hurdle that can only be surmounted by a level head.

Benefit 1:

Profit: The purpose that drives individuals into private business ventures is strictly profit. Profit is what capitalism is built on and it is what drives the real estate trade.

Benefit 2:

Self-employment: One of the great benefits of flipping homes is that you are your own boss. This means that you do not answer to anyone but yourself and the federal and state laws regulating house flipping, but mostly yourself.

Other benefits and risks involved I house flipping are listed and explained in the book in chapter 12.

Finally, buying and holding as an alternative to fast flipping is not to say that the latter is a better form of investment than the other. What this means that it is an alternative, a plan b for investors who would rather hold on to the property while the value appreciates and collecting equity in for of rents paid by tenants and then sells the property at any specific future date that satisfies the investor.

This book was written with the intention of informing the less informed about the workings, ups and downs, and activities that are involved in real estate transactions. While a lot of you would have bought or sold a house before, but what this book brings to the table is the knowledge of how to go about it professionally, if you so wish. It would be a wonderful tool in your utility belt as you saddle up and gird your loins to start investing in real estate.

Made in the USA
Monee, IL
19 August 2022

11965536R00118